VARIOU

Harold Pinter was born in London in 1930. He is married to Antonia Fraser. In 1995 he won the David Cohen British Literature Prize, awarded for a lifetime's achievement in literature.

HAROLD PINTER

Various Voices

PROSE, POETRY, POLITICS
1948–1998

faber and faber

First published in 1998
by Faber and Faber Limited
3 Queen Square London WC1N 3AU
This paperback edition first published in 1999

Photoset by Wilmaset Ltd, Birkenhead, Wirral
Printed in England by Mackays of Chatham PLC, Chatham, Kent

This collection © Harold Pinter, 1998

Harold Pinter is hereby identified as author of this
work in accordance with Section 77 of the Copyright,
Designs and Patents Act 1988

*This book is sold subject to the condition that it shall not,
by way of trade or otherwise, be lent, resold, hired out or
otherwise circulated without the publisher's prior consent in
any form of binding or cover other than that in which it is
published and without a similar condition including this
condition being imposed on the subsequent purchaser*

A CIP record for this book
is available from the British Library

ISBN 0-571-19728-0

2 4 6 8 10 9 7 5 3 1

Contents

[I]

A Note on Shakespeare

The mistake they make, most of them, is to attempt to determine and calculate, with the finest instruments, the source of the wound.

They seek out the gaps between the apparent and the void that hinges upon it with all due tautness. They turn to the wound with deference, a lance, and a needle and thread.

At the entrance of the lance the gap widens. At the use of needle and thread the wound coagulates and atrophies in their hands.

Shakespeare writes of the open wound and, through him, we know it open and know it closed. We tell when it ceases to beat and tell it at its highest peak of fever.

In attempting to approach Shakespeare's work in its entirety, you are called upon to grapple with a perspective in which the horizon alternately collapses and re-forms behind you, in which the mind is subject to an intense diversity of atmospheric.

Once the investigation has begun, however, there is no other way but to him.

One discovers a long corridor of postures; fluid and hardened at the quick; gross and godlike; putrescent and copulative; raddled; attentive; crippled and gargantuan; crumbling with the dropsy; heavy with elephantiasis; broody with government; severe; fanatical; paralytic; voluptuous; impassive; musclebound; lissom; virginal; unwashed; bewildered; humpbacked; icy and statuesque. All are contained in the wound which Shakespeare does not attempt to sew up or re-shape, whose pain he does not attempt to eradicate. He amputates, deadens, aggravates at will, within the limits of a particular piece, but he will not pronounce judgement or cure. Such comment as there is is so variously split up between characters and so contradictory in itself that no central point of opinion or inclining can be determined.

He himself is trapped in his own particular order, and is unable to go out at a distance to regulate and forestall abortion or lapses in vraisemblance. He can only rely on a 'few well chosen words' to bring him through any doubtful patch.

He belongs, of course, ultimately, to a secret society, a conspiracy, of which there is only one member: himself. In that sense, and in a number of others too, he is a malefactor; a lunatic; a deserter, a conscientious objector; a guttersnipe; a social menace and an Anti-Christ.

He is also a beggar; a road-sweeper; a tinker; a hashish-drinker; a leper; a chicken-fancier; a paper-seller; a male nurse; a sun-worshipper and a gibbering idiot.

He is no less a traffic policeman; a rowing blue; a rear-gunner; a chartered accountant; a best man; a bus-conductor; a paid guide; a marriage-guidance counsellor; a church-goer; a stage carpenter; an umpire; an acrobat and a clerk of the court.

His tongue is guttural, Arabic, pepperish, composed, parsimonious, voluminous, rabid, diarrhoeic, transparent, laundered, dainty, mellifluous, consonantal, stammering, scabrous, naked, blade-edged, one-legged, piercing, hushed, clinical, dumb, convulsed, lewd, vicious, voracious, inane, Tibetan, monosyllabic, epileptic, raucous, ministerial, sudden, Sudanese, palpitating, thunderous, earthy, whimsical, acrimonious, wintry, malicious, fearsome, blighted, blistered, mouldy, tantalizing, juicy, innocent, lordly, gluttonous, irreverent, blasphemous, avaricious, autumnal, blasted, ecstatic, necromantic, gentle, venomous, somnambulistic, monotonous, uproarious, feverish, austere, demented, deathly, fractious, obsessed, ironic, palsied, morbid, sanctimonious, sacrilegious, calm, cunning, cannibalistic and authoritative.

He moves through all with a vehement and flexible control.

He turns and bites his own tail. He defecates on his own carpet. He repeats the Bible sideways. He disdains the communication cord and the life-belt. He scratches his head with an iceberg. But the fabric never breaks. The tightrope is never at less than an even stretch. He aborts, he meanders, he loses his track, he overshoots his mark, he drops his glasses, he meets himself coming back, he digresses, he calumniates, he alters direction, he sinks in at the knees, he rolls over like a log, he forgets the drift, he drops someone flat, he exaggerates, oversimplifies, disrupts, falsifies, evades the issue, is carried home drunk; he dawdles, he dwindles, he trips over his own feet, he runs away with himself, he implicates others, he misses the point, he ends up at the same place, he falls back on geometry, he cheats, he squanders, he leaves it at that; he gets in his own way, he burns his fingers, he turns turtle, he stews in his own juice, he loses all hands; suffers fire, arsony, rape, loot, ravage, fraud, bondage, murder, interference, snobbery, lice, jealousy, snakebites, damp beds, falling arches, jugglery, quackery, mastoids, bunions, hailstones, bladder trouble, fainting fits, eye-strain, morning sickness, heat, dirt, riot, plague, suicide. He suffers, commits and survives them all.

The fabric never breaks. The wound is open. The wound is peopled.

1950

On *The Birthday Party* I

Letter to Peter Wood, director of *The Birthday Party*, written just before rehearsals started for the first production of the play in April 1958.

Dear Peter,

The first image of this play, the first thing that about a year ago was put on paper, was a kitchen, Meg, Stanley, corn flakes and sour milk. There they were, they sat, they stood, they bent, they turned, they were incontravertable, or perhaps I should say incontrovertible. Not long before Goldberg and McCann turned up. They had come with a purpose, a job in hand – to take Stanley away. This they did, Meg unknowing, Petey helpless, Stanley sucked in. Play over. That was the pure line and I couldn't get away from it. I had no idea at the time what or why. The thing germinated and bred itself. It proceeded according to its own logic. What did I do? I followed the indications, I kept a sharp eye on the clues I found myself dropping. The writing arranged itself with no trouble into dramatic terms. The characters sounded in my ears – it was apparent to me what one would say and what would be the other's response, at any given point. It was apparent to me what they would not, could not, ever, say, whatever one might wish. I interfered with them only on the technical level. My task was not to damage their consistency at any time – through any external notion of my own.

When the thing was well cooked I began to form certain conclusions. The point is, however, that by that time the play was now its own world. It was determined by its own original engendering image. My conclusions were only useful in that they were informed by the growth of the work itself. When I began to think *analytically* about it (as far as I can manage to do that, which isn't very far) I did so by keeping in step with what was being suggested, by judging the whole caper through an accurate assessment of the happenings described, or what I concluded was an accurate assessment. I never held up the work in hand to another mirror – I related it to nothing outside itself. Certainly to no other work of literature or to any consideration of public approbation should it reach a stage.

The play is itself. It is no other. It has its own life (whatever its merit in dramatic terms or accomplishment may be and despite the dissatisfaction others may experience with regard to it). I take it you would like me to insert a clarification or moral judgement or author's angle on it, straight from the horse's mouth. I appreciate your desire for this but I can't do it.

I confused the issue by talking of what 'I thought' of the characters. Who I would invite to tea, etc. That's irrelevant. The play exists now apart from me, you or anybody. I believe that what happens on this stage will possess a potent dramatic image and a great deal of this will be visual – I mean one will *see* the people, which will be a great aid to the expression of the thing, the getting across. The curtain goes up and comes down. Something has happened. Right? Cock-eyed, brutish, absurd, with no comment. Where is the comment, the slant, the explanatory note? In the play. Everything to do with the play is in the play.

All right. You know what I think about Stanley. I think he has the right, whatever he does and is, to do and be just that and fuck the expense. That's what I think. But that is not the point of the play. It is a conclusion I draw from it. Is that *a* point expressed in the play? Only by implication, agreed. I conclude what I conclude upon that implication. Stanley fights for his life, he doesn't want to be drowned. Who does? But he is not *articulate*. The play in fact merely states that two men come down to take away another man and do so. Will the audience absorb the implications or will they not? Ask the barber.

Audience reaction, it seems to me, might be one of three –
(a) They should have left him alone. (b) The silly bugger
deserved it. (c) It's all a load of crap. There is also, of course,
(d) How fascinating, but what does it mean? To which I reply
– Meaning begins in the words, in the action, continues in
your head and ends nowhere. There is no end to meaning.
Meaning which is resolved, parcelled, labelled and ready for
export is dead, impertinent – and meaningless. I examine my
own play and ask, what's going on here? I note – this seems to
lead from that, I would conclude this, but the characters
themselves do nothing but move through an occurrence, a
morning, a night, a morning. This occurrence has, admittedly,
any number of implications. Anyone is entitled to see the
show. The dramatic progression and the implications implicit
in it will either find a home in some part of their nut or not.

To put such words as we discussed into Stanley's mouth
would be an inexcusable imposition and falsity on my part.
Stanley *cannot* perceive his only valid justification – which is,
he is what he is – therefore he certainly can never be articulate
about it. He knows only to attempt to justify himself by
dream, by pretence and by bluff, through fright. If he had
cottoned on to the fact that he need only admit to himself
what he actually is and is not – then Goldberg and McCann
would not have paid their visit, or if they had, the same course
of events would have been by no means assured. Stanley
would have been another man. The play would have been
another play. A play with a 'sensitive intellectual' articulate
hero in its centre, able to examine himself in any way clearly,
would also have been another play.

Stanley is the king of his castle and loses his kingdom
because he assessed it and himself inaccurately. We all have to
be very careful. The boot is itching to squash and very
efficient.

Goldberg and McCann? Dying, rotting, scabrous, the
decayed spiders, the flower of our society. They know their
way around. Our mentors. Our ancestry. Them. Fuck 'em.

What would you, as they say? In the third act Stanley can do nothing but make a noise. What else? What else has he discovered? He has been reduced to the fact that he is nothing but a gerk in the throat. But does this sound signify anything? It might very well. I think it does. He is trying to go further. He is on the edge of utterance. But it's a long, impossible edge and utterance, were he to succeed in falling into it, might very well prove to be only one cataclysmic, profound fart. You think I'm joking? Test me. In the rattle in his throat Stanley approximates nearer to the true nature of himself than ever before and certainly ever after. But it is late. Late in the day. He can go no further.

At that juncture, you will appreciate, he cannot be expected to suddenly recover the old gift of the gab and speak a set piece of self-analysis or self-realization, to point a tiny little moral. Nor could he earlier in the play for it would never occur to him to justify himself in that manner. Nor, for instance, could Petey in his last chat with Goldberg and McCann deliver the thought for today or the what we learn from these nasty experiences homily since, apart from anything else, we are not dealing with an articulate household and there is no Chorus in this play. In other words, I am afraid I do not find myself disposed to add a programme note to this piece.

None of what I have said means that I disclaim responsibility for my characters. On the contrary, I am responsible both for them and to them. The play dictated itself but I confess that I wrote it – with intent, maliciously, purposefully, in command of its growth. Does this appear to contradict all I said earlier? Splendid. You may suggest that this 'command' was not strict enough and not lucid enough but who supposes I'm striving for lucidity? I think the house is in pretty good order. We've agreed; the hierarchy, the Establishment, the arbiters, the socio-religious monsters arrive to effect alteration and censure upon a member of the club who has discarded responsibility (that word again) towards himself and others. (What is your opinion, by the way, of the act of suicide?) He does possess, however, for my money, a certain fibre – he fights for his life. It doesn't last long, this fight. His core being a quagmire of delusion, his mind a tenuous fusebox, he collapses under the weight of their accusation – an accusation compounded of the shitstained strictures of centuries of 'tradition'. Though nonconformist, he is neither hero nor exemplar of revolt. Nothing salutary for the audience to identify itself with. And *yet*, at the same time, I believe that a greater degree of identification will take place than might seem likely. A great deal, it seems to me, will depend on the actor. If he copes with Stanley's loss of himself successfully, I believe a certain amount of poignancy will emanate. Couldn't we all find ourselves in Stanley's position at any given moment?

As for the practical question of the end of Act Two, where's the difficulty? Stanley behaves strangely. Why? Because his alteration-diminution has set in, he is rendered offcock (not off cock), he has lost any adult comprehension and reverts to a childhood malice and mischief, as his first shelter. This is the beginning of his change, his fall. In the third act we see the next phase.

The play is a comedy because the whole state of affairs is absurd and inglorious. It is, however, as you know, a very serious piece of work.

A simple matter, don't you think?

Yours,

Harold Pinter

Note by Martin Esslin, editor of the *Kenyon Review*

The Birthday Party was Harold Pinter's first full-length play. It opened its out-of-town try-out run at the Arts Theatre in Cambridge on 28 April 1958, came to the Lyric Theatre, Hammersmith, in London on 19 May and closed on 24 May, having, in that fairly large house, taken only a grand total of two hundred and sixty pounds, eleven shillings and eight pence for the whole week's run.

Like all truly original and innovative works of art, the play bewildered and disconcerted its audience and – as we can see from Harold Pinter's letter to the director printed here – its director and actors as well. *The Birthday Party* seemed to many members of its first audiences to start off as a thriller, a mystery play; but, then, it failed to keep its promise: it provided no solution to the mystery. What had Stanley, that amiable but weak young man, done to make him hide away in a sleazy seaside boarding-house, where he was being mothered by a possessive elderly landlady; and what brought the two sinister agents to seek him out: the archetypal Jewish swindler Goldberg and the equally archetypal Irish terrorist McCann? And why were these two arranging what they termed a birthday party for Stanley, during which they brainwashed and tormented him? And where did they take him away, having broken his glasses and thus having blinded him and reduced him to speechlessness, in a big black car?

All this was puzzling. It was clear that a major talent was at work: the brilliance and wit of the dialogue, the sharpness of its clinical observation of the quirks and idiocies of real speech, the subtle syncopation of its rhythms and the transition from its realism to wilder and wilder regions of surrealist free association clearly marked the author as a virtuoso of stage language. But what was he trying to say in the play?

Pinter himself, at the time, steadfastly – and rightly – refused to be tempted into self-explanation and commentary on himself. It is not for an artist to provide a critical child's guide to his intentions. A work of art must speak for itself.

And, of course, some critics gradually succeeded in providing approaches to explanations, avenues towards an understanding of the play's meaning: that it was an image of a *mood* rather than an attempt to tell a story; that it combined a number of equally viable allegorical meanings that worked precisely because they were all equally true; that the very lack of explanation was the main image of the play: a metaphor for the inexplicable uncertainties and mysteries of the human condition itself, with its transitions from one stage of existence to another, youth to age, life to death.

Now, almost a quarter of a century after *The Birthday Party* startled its audience, Harold Pinter has agreed to the publication of the letter he wrote to the director of its first production. It is an important document. It is also a very fine piece of expository prose.

Martin Esslin, 1981

On *The Birthday Party* II

Letter to the Editor of *The Play's the Thing*,
October 1958

Thank you for your invitation to make a few observations in your magazine about writing for the stage, with reference to the rise and fall of my play, *The Birthday Party*. Your columns are more congenial to me than most since yours is an inter-university paper and the response given to *The Birthday Party* in Oxford and in Cambridge was most stimulating, involving a high degree of participation on the part of both audiences. My contact with universities in this field has in fact always proved worthwhile. *The Room*, my first play, was originally produced by Henry Woolf at the Bristol University Drama Department. Not only the integrity and clarity of Mr Woolf's production but the enthusiasm of the whole group and the reception given the play there was highly encouraging and directly responsible for my further efforts in this medium. I have never been to a university myself. It would appear, however, that some communication takes place between my work and a university public. That is enough for me to recommend university life to others.

The remarkable difference in reaction to *The Birthday Party* on the part of the London daily paper critics and the audiences in Oxford and Cambridge constitutes for me one of the most interesting features of the progress of the play. (There was, of course, no audience in London; the abstention counselled by nine or eleven critics was heeded sufficiently to bring about the abrupt closure.) There is no glib deduction to be made from this wide divergence in reception. I tend to believe, however, that even where unfavourable, the response of the public in Oxford and Cambridge gave evidence of an active and willing intelligence brought into the theatre, not merely, as is usual, that brought by isolated individuals, but that of an audience alive. The weeks in these towns were exciting for the actors, the producer, the management, and for me. The week in London, following these, was a most curious kind of a week altogether. The simple answer to this state of affairs might be too simple. Perhaps it has something to do with the subtleties and distinctions of climate obtaining in different areas of the country? Impossible to say.

You have asked me if I acknowledge or refute the influence of Ionesco. At the time of writing *The Birthday Party* I knew only *The New Tenant* of Ionesco, and so can hardly consider myself working under his influence. It is, I suggest, legitimate to hold that a writer writing in Southend and a writer writing in Inverness may be found to have something in common without their having had an intimate knowledge of each other's work. This occurs, I think, more often than those obsessed by that most facile of things, the category, would care to recognize.

You have asked me to discuss the lines I myself am working on. I think I proceed from one or two simple assumptions in writing for the stage. Given a man in a room and he will sooner or later receive a visitor. A visitor entering the room will enter with intent. If two people inhabit the room the visitor will not be the same man for both. A man in a room who receives a visit is likely to be illuminated or horrified by it. The visitor himself might as easily be horrified or illuminated. The man may leave with the visitor or he may leave alone. The visitor may leave alone or stay in the room alone when the man is gone. Or they may both stay together in the room. Whatever the outcome in terms of movement, the original condition, in which a man sat alone in a room, will have been subjected to alteration. A man in a room and no one entering lives in expectation of a visit. He will be illuminated or horrified by the absence of a visitor. But however much it is expected, the entrance, when it comes, is unexpected and almost always unwelcome. (He himself, of course, might go out of the door, knock and come in and be his own visitor. It has happened before.)

Not by any means everyone can be moved from his delusion. Where this is going to occur it will occur shockingly. It may induce paralysis. From paralysis to paralysis. Or from delusion to delusion. For if the intention of the visitor is to strip the man of his delusion, and if this is successful, he may then clothe the man in one of his own, on the principle that delusions are adjustable and can be worn by anybody. You can wear mine. I can wear yours. All you have to do is give me time for a fitting. On the other hand, given these ingredients of man and visitor, something quite different might take place; what could be called a liberation. A great deal will depend, of course, on what kind of man the visitor is, on his personality, so to speak. What is certain is that an adjustment of some magnitude will be necessary, either to a condition beneficial to the mind and disposition of the person concerned, or to one detrimental.

When I speak of a visitor I do not mean 'A Visitor', an avenging angel, a messenger of Death, Doom, heaven or the Milky Way. A character will certainly reflect inherited attitudes and attributes. By inference or implication his allegiances may be located. This does not necessarily mean that he is a direct representation of any particular 'force'. When a character cannot be comfortably defined or understood in terms of the familiar the tendency is to perch him on a symbolic shelf, out of harm's way. Once there, he can be talked about but need not be lived with. To postulate that what is unfamiliar bears no direct relation to experience is to forget that what is unfamiliar is not necessarily unrecognizable. While much of what is recognizable certainly remains unrecognized, this does not make it any the less recognizable at a given time and under certain given conditions.

We all have our function. The visitor will have his. There is no guarantee, however, that he will possess a visiting card, with detailed information as to his last place of residence, last job, next job, number of dependants, etc. Nor, for the comfort of all, an identity card, nor a label on his chest. The desire for verification is understandable but cannot always be satisfied. There are no hard distinctions between what is real and what is unreal, nor between what is true and what is false. A thing is not necessarily either true or false; it can be both true and false. The assumption that to verify what has happened and what is happening presents few problems I take to be inaccurate. A character on the stage who can present no convincing argument or information as to his past experience, his present behaviour or his aspirations, nor give a comprehensive analysis of his motives is as legitimate and as worthy of attention as one who, alarmingly, can do all these things. The more acute the experience the less articulate its expression.

I am sure that readers of your magazine fully acknowledge the double, treble, quadruple life lived under the term life. A play is not an essay, nor can a playwright under any exhortation damage the consistency of his characters by injecting a remedy or apology for their actions into the third act, simply because we have been brought up to expect, rain or sunshine, the third act 'resolution'. To supply an explicit moral tag to an evolving and compulsive dramatic image seems to me facile, impertinent and dishonest. Where this takes place it is not theatre but a crossword puzzle. The audience holds the paper. The play fills in the blanks. Everyone's happy. There has been no conflict between audience and play, no participation, nothing has been exposed. We walk out as we went in. In Oxford and Cambridge with *The Birthday Party* I felt this was not the case. The audience was active and involved. This activity and involvement was to me most gratifying.

Writing for the Theatre

A speech made by Harold Pinter at the National Student Drama Festival in Bristol in 1962

I'm not a theorist. I'm not an authoritative or reliable commentator on the dramatic scene, the social scene, any scene. I write plays, when I can manage it, and that's all. That's the sum of it. So I'm speaking with some reluctance, knowing that there are at least twenty-four possible aspects of any single statement, depending on where you're standing at the time or on what the weather's like. A categorical statement, I find, will never stay where it is and be finite. It will immediately be subject to modification by the other twenty-three possibilities of it. No statement I make, therefore, should be interpreted as final and definitive. One or two of them may sound final and definitive, they may even be *almost* final and definitive, but I won't regard them as such tomorrow and I wouldn't like you to do so today.

I've had two full-length plays produced in London. The first ran a week and the second ran a year. Of course, there are differences between the two plays. In *The Birthday Party* I employed a certain amount of dashes in the text, between phrases. In *The Caretaker* I cut out the dashes and used dots instead. So that instead of, say: 'Look, dash, who, dash, I, dash, dash, dash,' the text would read: 'Look, dot, dot, dot, who, dot, dot, dot, I, dot, dot, dot, dot.' So it's possible to deduce from this that dots are more popular than dashes and that's why *The Caretaker* had a longer run than *The Birthday Party*. The fact that in neither case could you hear the dots and dashes in performance is beside the point. You can't fool the critics for long. They can tell a dot from a dash a mile off, even if they can hear neither.

It took me quite a while to grow used to the fact that

critical and public response in the theatre follows a very erratic temperature chart. And the danger for a writer is where he becomes easy prey for the old bugs of apprehension and expectation in this connection. But I think Düsseldorf cleared the air for me. In Düsseldorf about two years ago I took, as is the Continental custom, a bow with a German cast of *The Caretaker* at the end of the play on the first night. I was at once booed violently by what must have been the finest collection of booers in the world. I thought they were using megaphones, but it was pure mouth. The cast was as dogged as the audience, however, and we took thirty-four curtain calls, all to boos. By the thirty-fourth there were only two people left in the house, still booing. I was strangely warmed by all this, and now, whenever I sense a tremor of the old apprehension or expectation, I remember Düsseldorf, and am cured.

The theatre is a large, energetic, public activity. Writing is, for me, a completely private activity, a poem or a play, no difference. These facts are not easy to reconcile. The professional theatre, whatever the virtues it undoubtedly possesses, is a world of false climaxes, calculated tensions, some hysteria, and a good deal of inefficiency. And the alarms of this world which I suppose I work in become steadily more widespread and intrusive. But basically my position has remained the same. What I write has no obligation to anything other than to itself. My responsibility is not to audiences, critics, producers, directors, actors or to my fellow men in general, but to the play in hand, simply. I warned you about definitive statements but it looks as though I've just made one.

I have usually begun a play in quite a simple manner; found a couple of characters in a particular context, thrown them together and listened to what they said, keeping my nose to the ground. The context has always been, for me, concrete and particular, and the characters concrete also. I've never started a play from any kind of abstract idea or theory ...

Apart from any other consideration, we are faced with the immense difficulty, if not the impossibility, of verifying the past. I don't mean merely years ago, but yesterday, this morning. What took place, what was the nature of what took place, what happened? If one can speak of the difficulty of knowing what in fact took place yesterday, one can I think treat the present in the same way. What's happening now? We won't know until tomorrow or in six months' time, and we won't know then, we'll have forgotten, or our imagination will have attributed quite false characteristics to today. A moment is sucked away and distorted, often even at the time of its birth. We will all interpret a common experience quite differently, though we prefer to subscribe to the view that there's a shared common ground, a known ground. I think there's a shared common ground all right, but that it's more like a quicksand. Because 'reality' is quite a strong firm word we tend to think, or to hope, that the state to which it refers is equally firm, settled and unequivocal. It doesn't seem to be, and in my opinion, it's no worse or better for that.

[...]

... There is a considerable body of people just now who are asking for some kind of clear and sensible engagement to be evidently disclosed in contemporary plays. They want the playwright to be a prophet. There is certainly a good deal of prophecy indulged in by playwrights these days, in their plays and out of them. Warnings, sermons, admonitions, ideological exhortations, moral judgements, defined problems with built-in solutions; all can camp under the banner of prophecy. The attitude behind this sort of thing might be summed up in one phrase: 'I'm telling you!'

It takes all sorts of playwrights to make a world, and as far as I'm concerned 'X' can follow any course he chooses without my acting as his censor. To propagate a phoney war between hypothetical schools of playwrights doesn't seem to me a very productive pastime and it certainly isn't my intention. But I can't but feel that we have a marked tendency to stress, so glibly, our empty preferences. The preference for 'Life' with a capital L, which is held up to be very different to life with a small l, I mean the life we in fact live. The preference for goodwill, for charity, for benevolence, how facile they've become, these deliverances.

If I were to state any moral precept it might be: beware of the writer who puts forward his concern for you to embrace, who leaves you in no doubt of his worthiness, his usefulness, his altruism, who declares that his heart is in the right place, and ensures that it can be seen in full view, a pulsating mass where his characters ought to be. What is presented, so much of the time, as a body of active and positive thought is in fact a body lost in a prison of empty definition and cliché.

This kind of writer clearly trusts words absolutely. I have mixed feelings about words myself. Moving among them, sorting them out, watching them appear on the page, from this I derive a considerable pleasure. But at the same time I have another strong feeling about words which amounts to nothing less than nausea. Such a weight of words confronts us day in, day out, words spoken in a context such as this, words written by me and by others, the bulk of it a stale dead terminology; ideas endlessly repeated and permutated, become platitudinous, trite, meaningless. Given this nausea, it's very easy to be overcome by it and step back into paralysis. I imagine most writers know something of this kind of paralysis. But if it is possible to confront this nausea, to follow it to its hilt, to move through it and out of it, then it is possible to say that something has occurred, that something has even been achieved.

Language, under these conditions, is a highly ambiguous business. So often, below the word spoken, is the thing known and unspoken. My characters tell me so much and no more, with reference to their experience, their aspirations, their motives, their history. Between my lack of biographical data about them and the ambiguity of what they say lies a territory which is not only worthy of exploration but which it is compulsory to explore. You and I, the characters which grow on a page, most of the time we're inexpressive, giving little away, unreliable, elusive, evasive, obstructive, unwilling. But it's out of these attributes that a language arises. A language, I repeat, where under what is said, another thing is being said.

Given characters who possess a momentum of their own, my job is not to impose upon them, not to subject them to a false articulation, by which I mean forcing a character to speak where he could not speak, making him speak in a way he could not speak, or making him speak of what he could never speak. The relationship between author and characters should be a highly respectful one, both ways. And if it's possible to talk of gaining a kind of freedom from writing, it doesn't come by leading one's characters into fixed and calculated postures, but by allowing them to carry their own can, by giving them legitimate elbowroom. This can be extremely painful. It's much easier, much less pain, not to let them live.

I'd like to make quite clear at the same time that I don't regard my own characters as uncontrolled or anarchic. They're not. The function of selection and arrangement is mine. I do all the donkeywork, in fact, and I think I can say I pay meticulous attention to the shape of things, from the shape of a sentence to the overall structure of the play. This shaping is of the first importance. But I think a double thing happens. You arrange *and* you listen, following the clues you leave for yourself, through the characters. And sometimes a balance is found, where image can freely engender image and where at the same time you are able to keep your sights on the place where the characters are silent and in hiding. It is in the silence that they are most evident to me.

There are two silences. One when no word is spoken. The other when perhaps a torrent of language is being employed. This speech is speaking of a language locked beneath it. That is its continual reference. The speech we hear is an indication of that which we don't hear. It is a necessary avoidance, a violent, sly, anguished or mocking smoke screen which keeps the other in its place. When true silence falls we are still left with echo but are nearer nakedness. One way of looking at speech is to say that it is a constant stratagem to cover nakedness.

We have heard many times that tired, grimy phrase: 'failure of communication' ... and this phrase has been fixed to my work quite consistently. I believe the contrary. I think that we communicate only too well, in our silence, in what is unsaid, and that what takes place is a continual evasion, desperate rearguard attempts to keep ourselves to ourselves. Communication is too alarming. To enter into someone else's life is too frightening. To disclose to others the poverty within us is too fearsome a possibility.

I am not suggesting that no character in a play can ever say what he in fact means. Not at all. I have found that there invariably does come a moment when this happens, when he says something, perhaps, which he has never said before. And where this happens, what he says is irrevocable, and can never be taken back.

A blank page is both an exciting and a frightening thing. It's what you start from. There follow two further periods in the progress of a play. The rehearsal period and the performance. A dramatist will absorb a great many things of value from an active and intense experience in the theatre, throughout these two periods. But finally he is again left looking at the blank page. In that page is something or nothing. You don't know until you've covered it. And there's no guarantee that you will know then. But it always remains a chance worth taking.

I've written nine plays, for various media, and at the moment I haven't the slightest idea how I've managed to do it. Each play was, for me, 'a different kind of failure'. And that fact, I suppose, sent me on to write the next one.

And if I find writing plays an extremely difficult task, while still understanding it as a kind of celebration, how much more difficult it is to attempt to rationalize the process, and how much more abortive, as I think I've clearly demonstrated to you this morning.

Samuel Beckett says, at the beginning of his novel *The Unnamable*, 'The fact would seem to be, if in my situation one may speak of facts, not only that I shall have to speak of things of which I cannot speak, but also, which is even more interesting, but also that I, which is if possible even more interesting, that I shall have to, I forget, no matter.'

Mac

Anew McMaster was born in County Monaghan on Christmas Eve 1894 and was sixteen when he made his first stage appearance as 'The Aristocrat' in *The Scarlet Pimpernel* with Fred Terry at the New Theatre, London. He died in Dublin on 25 August 1962, a few days after appearing in the 'dream scene' from *The Bells* at an Equity concert. His acting career had spanned half a century and his death was the end of an era. He was the last of the great actor-managers, unconnected with films and television.

I've been the toast of twelve continents and eight hemispheres! Mac said from his hotel bed. I'll see none of my admirers before noon. Marjorie, where are my teeth? His teeth were brought to him. None before noon, he said, and looked out of the window. If the clergy call say I am studying *King Lear* and am not to be disturbed. How long have you been studying *King Lear*, Mac? Since I was a boy. I can play the part. It's the lines I can't learn. That's the problem. The part I can do. I think. What do you think? Do you think I can do it? I wonder if I'm wise to want to do it, or unwise? But I will do it. I'll do it next season.

Don't forget I was acclaimed for my performance in *Paddy the Next Best Thing*. Never forget that. Should I take *Othello* to the Embassy, Swiss Cottage? Did you know Godfrey Tearle left out the fit? He didn't do the fit. I'm older than Godfrey Tearle. But I do the fit. Don't I? At least I don't leave it out. What's your advice? Should I take *Othello* to the Embassy, Swiss Cottage? Look out the window at this town. What a stinking diseased abandoned Godforgotten bog. What am I playing tonight, Marjorie? *The Taming of the Shrew*? But you see one thing the Irish peasantry really appreciate is style, grace and wit. You have a lovely company, someone said to me the other day, a lovely company, all the boys is like girls. Joe, are the posters up? Will we pack out? I was just driving into the town and I had to brake at a dung heap. A cow looked in through the window. No autographs today, I said. Let's have a drop of whiskey, for Jesus' sake.

Pat Magee phoned me from Ireland to tell me Mac was dead. I decided to go to the funeral. At London Airport the plane was very late leaving. I hadn't been in Ireland for ten years. The taxi raced through Dublin. We passed the Sinn Fein Hall, where we used to rehearse five plays in two weeks. But I knew I was too late for the funeral. The cemetery was empty. I saw no one I knew. I didn't know Mrs Mac's address. I knew no one any more in Dublin. I couldn't find Mac's grave.

I toured Ireland with Mac for about two years in the early 1950s. He advertised in *The Stage* for actors for a Shakespearian tour of the country. I sent him a photograph and went to see him in a flat near Willesden Junction. At the time Willesden Junction seemed to me as likely a place as any to meet a manager from whom you might get work. But after I knew Mac our first meeting place became more difficult to accept or understand. I still wonder what he was doing interviewing actors at Willesden Junction. But I never asked him. He offered me six pounds a week, said I could get digs for twenty-five shillings at the most, told me how cheap cigarettes were and that I could play Horatio, Bassanio and Cassio. It was my first job proper on the stage.

Those two? It must be like two skeletons copulating on a bed of corrugated iron. (The actor and actress Mac was talking about were very thin.) He undercuts me, he said, he keeps coming in under me. I'm the one who should come under. I'm playing Hamlet. But how can I play Hamlet if he keeps coming under me all the time? The more under I go the more under he goes. Nobody in the audience can hear a word. The bugger wants to play Hamlet himself, that's what it is. But he bloodywell won't while I'm alive. When I die I hope I die quickly. I couldn't face months of bedpans. Sheer hell. Days and months of bedpans. Do you think we'll go to heaven? I mean me. Do you think I'll go to heaven? You never saw me play the Cardinal. My cloak was superb, the length of the stage, crimson. I had six boys from the village to carry it. They used to kiss my ring every night before we made our entrance. When I made my tour of Australia and the southern hemisphere we were the guests of honour at a city banquet. The Mayor stood up. He said: We are honoured today to welcome to our city one of the most famous actors in the world, an actor who has given tremendous pleasure to people all over the world, to worldwide acclaim. It is my great privilege to introduce to you – Andrew MacPherson!

Joe Nolan, the business manager, came in one day and said: Mac, all the cinemas in Limerick are on strike. What shall I do? Book Limerick! Mac said. At once! We'll open on Monday. There was no theatre in the town. We opened on the Monday in a two thousand seater cinema, with *Othello*. There was no stage and no wingspace. It was St Patrick's night. The curtain was supposed to rise at nine o'clock. But the house wasn't full until eleven thirty, so the play didn't begin until then. It was well past two in the morning before the curtain came down. Every one of the two thousand people in the audience was drunk. Apart from that, they weren't accustomed to Shakespeare. For the first half of the play, up to 'I am your own for ever', we could not hear ourselves speak, could not hear our cues. The cast was alarmed. We expected the audience on stage at any moment. We kept our hands on our swords. I was playing Iago at the time. I came offstage with Mac at the interval and gasped. Don't worry, Mac said, don't worry. After the interval he began to move. When he walked on to the stage for the 'Naked in bed, Iago, and not mean harm' scene (his great body hunched, his voice low with grit), they silenced. He tore into the fit. He made the play his and the place his. By the time he had reached 'It is the very error of the moon; She comes more near the earth than she was wont, And makes men mad' (the word 'mad' suddenly cauterized, ugly, shocking), the audience was quite still. And sober. I congratulated Mac. Not bad, he said, was it? Not bad. Godfrey Tearle never did the fit, you know.

Mac gave about half a dozen magnificent performances of Othello while I was with him. Even when, on the other occasions, he conserved his energies in the role, he always gave the patrons their moneysworth. At his best his was the finest Othello I have seen. His age was always a mystery, but I would think he was in his sixties at the time. Sometimes, late at night, after the show, he looked very old. But on stage in *Othello* he stood, well over six foot, naked to the waist, his gestures complete, final, nothing jagged, his movement of the utmost fluidity and yet of the utmost precision: stood there, dead in the centre of the role, and the great sweeping symphonic playing would begin, the rare tension and release within him, the arrest, the swoop, the savagery, the majesty and repose. His voice was unique: in my experience of an unequalled range. A bass of extraordinary echo, resonance and gut, and remarkable sweep up into tenor, when the note would hit the back of the gallery and come straight back, a brilliant, stunning sound. I remember his delivery of this line: 'Methinks (bass) it should be now a huge (bass) eclipse (tenor) of sun and moon (baritone) and that th'affrighted glove (bass) Should yawn (very deep, the abyss) at alteration.' We all watched him from the wings.

He was capable, of course, of many indifferent and offhand performances. On these occasions an edgy depression and fatigue hung over him. He would gabble his way through the part, his movement fussed, his voice acting outside him, the man himself detached from its acrobatics. At such times his eyes would fix upon the other actors, appraising them coldly, emanating a grim dissatisfaction with himself and his company. Afterwards, over a drink, he would confide: I was bad tonight, wasn't I, really awful, but the damn cast was even worse. What a lot.

He was never a good Hamlet and for some reason or other rarely bothered to play Macbeth. He was obsessed with the lighting in *Macbeth* and more often than not spent half his time on stage glaring at the spot bar. Yet there was plenty of Macbeth in him. I believe his dislike of the play was so intense he couldn't bring himself to play it.

It was consistent with him that after many months of coasting through Shylock he suddenly lashed fullfired into the role at an obscure matinée in a onehorse village; a frightening performance. Afterwards he said to me: What did I do? Did you notice? I did something different. What did you think of it? What was it I did? He never did it again. Not quite like that. Who saw it?

In the trial scene in *The Merchant of Venice* one night I said to him (as Bassanio) instead of 'For thy three thousand ducats here is six', quite involuntarily, 'For thy three thousand *buckets* here is six.' He replied quietly and with emphasis: 'If every *bucket* in six thousand *buckets* were in six parts, and every part a *bucket* I would not draw them – I would have my bond.' I could not continue. The other members of the court scene and I turned upstage. Some walked into the wings. But Mac stood, remorseless, grave, like an eagle, waiting for my reply.

Sometimes after a matinée of *Macbeth* and an evening of *Othello* we all stayed on stage, he'd get someone to put on a record of *Faust*, disappear behind a curtain, reappear in a long golden wig, without his teeth, mime Marguerite weaving, mime Faust and Mephistopheles, deliver at full tilt the aria from Verdi's *Othello* 'Era la notte e Cassio dormia', while the caretaker swept the dust up, and then in a bar talk for hours of Sarah and Mrs Pat Campbell, with relish, malice and devotion. I think he would still be talking about them now, if he wasn't dead, because they did something he knew about.

In order to present *Oedipus* the company had to recruit extras from the town or village we were in. One night in Dundalk Mac was building up to his blind climax when one of the extras had an epileptic fit on stage and collapsed. He was dragged to the wings where various women attended to him. The sounds of their ministrations seeped on to the stage. Mac stopped, turned to the wings and shouted: 'For God's sake, can't you see I'm trying to act!'

His concentration was always complete in *Oedipus*. He was at his best in the part. He acted with acute 'underness' and tenacity. And he never used his vocal powers to better or truer effect. He acted along the spine of the role and never deviated from it. As in his two other great roles, Othello and Lear, he understood and expressed totally the final tender clarity which is under the storm, the blindness, the anguish. For me his acting at these times embodied the idea of Yeats' line: 'They know that Hamlet and Lear are gay, Gaiety transfiguring all that dread'. Mac entered into this tragic gaiety naturally and inevitably.

He did *Lear* eventually. First performance somewhere in County Clare, Ennis, I think. Knew most of the lines. *Was* the old man, tetchy, appalled, feverish. Wanted the storm louder. All of us banged the thundersheets. No, they can still hear me. Hit it, hit it. He got above the noise. I played Edgar in *Lear* only a few times with him before I left the company.

At the centre of his performance was a terrible loss, desolation, silence. He didn't think about doing it, he just got there. He did it and got there.

His wife, Marjorie, was his structure and support. She organized the tours, supervised all business arrangements, sat in the box office, kept the cast in order, ran the wardrobe, sewed, looked after Mac, was his dresser, gave him his whiskey. She was tough, critical, cultivated, devoted. Her spirit and belief constituted the backbone of the company. There would have been no company without her.

Ireland wasn't golden always, but it was golden sometimes and in 1950 it was, all in all, a golden age for me and for others.

The people came down to see him. Mac travelled by car, and sometimes some of us did too. But other times we went on the lorry with the flats and props, and going into Bandon or Cloughjordan would find the town empty, asleep, men sitting upright in dark bars, cow-pads, mud, smell of peat, wood, old clothes. We'd find digs; wash basin and jug, tea, black pudding, and off to the hall, set up a stage on trestle tables, a few rostra, a few drapes, costumes out of the hampers, set up shop, and at night play, not always but mostly, to a packed house (where had they come from?); people who listened, and who waited to see him, having seen him before, and been brought up on him.

Mac wasn't any kind of dreamer. He was remote from the Celtic Twilight. He kept a close eye on the box office receipts. He was sharp about money, was as depressed as anyone else when business was bad. Where there was any kind of company disagreement he proved elusive. He distanced himself easily from unwelcome problems. Mrs Mac dealt with those. Mac was never 'a darling actor of the old school'. He was a working man. He respected his occupation and never stopped learning about it, from himself and from others.

For those who cared for him and admired him there must remain one great regret; that for reasons I do not understand, he last played in England, at Stratford, in 1933. The loser was the English theatre.

Mac wasn't 'childlike' in temperament, as some have said. He was evasive, proud, affectionate, mischievous, shrewd, merry, cynical, sad and could be callous. But he was never sour or selfpitying. His life was the stage. Life with a big L came a bad second. He had no patience with what he considered a world of petty sufferings, however important they might seem to the bearer. He was completely unsentimental. Gossip delighted him, and particularly sexual gossip. He moved with great flexibility and amusement through Catholic Ireland, greatly attracted by the ritual of the Church. He loved to speak of the mummy of the Blessed Oliver Plunkett in Drogheda 'with a lovely amber spot on its face'. He mixed freely with priests and nuns, went to Mass, sometimes, but despised the religious atrophy, rigidity and complacency with which he was confronted. He mixed with the priests partly because he enjoyed their company, partly because his livelihood depended upon them. He was a realist. But he possessed a true liberality of spirit. He was humble. He was a devout anti-puritan. He was a very great piss-taker. He was a great actor and we who worked with him were the luckiest people in the world and loved him.

1966

Hutton and the Past

Hardstaff and Simpson at Lord's. Notts versus Middlesex. 1946 or 1947. After lunch, Keeton and Harris had opened for Notts. Keeton swift, exact, interested; Harris Harris. Harris stonewalled five balls in the over for no particular reason and hit the sixth for six, for no particular reason. Keeton and Harris gave Notts a fair start. Stott, at number three, smacked the ball hard, was out in the early afternoon. Simpson joined Hardstaff. Both very upright in their stance. They surveyed the field, surveyed themselves, began to bat.

The sun was strong, but calm. They settled into the afternoon, no hurry, all in order. Hardstaff clipped to mid-wicket. They crossed. Simpson guided the ball between midoff and the bowler. They crossed. Their cross was a trot, sometimes a walk, they didn't need to run. They placed their shots with precision, they knew where they were going. Bareheaded. Hardstaff golden. Simpson dark. Hardstaff offdrove, silently, Simpson to deep square leg. Simpson cut. Hardstaff cut, finer. Simpson finer. The slips, Robertson, Bennett, attentive. Hardstaff hooked, immaculate, no sound. They crossed, and back. Deep square leg in the heat after it. Jim Sims on at the pavilion end with leg breaks. Hardstaff wristed him into the covers. Simpson to fine leg. Two. Sims twisting. Hardstaff wristed him into the covers, through the covers, fielder wheeling, for four. Quite unhurried. Seventy in ninety minutes. No explosions. Batsmanship. Hardstaff caught at slip, off Sims.

Worrell and Weekes at Kingston on Thames 1950. The Festival. Headley had flicked, showed what had been and what remained of himself, from the thirties. Worrell joined Weekes with an hour to play. Gladwin and Jackson bowling. Very tight, very crisp, just short of a length, jolting, difficult. Worrell and Weekes scored ninety before close of play. No sixes, nothing off the ground. Weekes smashed, red-eyed, past cover, smashed to long leg, at war, met Gladwin head on, split midwicket in two, steel. Worrell wanted to straight drive to reach his fifty. Four men at the sight screen to stop him. He straight drove, pierced them, reached his fifty. Gladwin bowled a stinging ball, only just short, on middle and leg. Only sensible course was to stop it. Worrell jumped up, both feet off, slashed it from his stomach, square cut for four, boundary first bounce.

MCC versus Australians. Lord's 1948. Monday. On the Saturday the Australians had plastered the MCC bowling. Barnes 100, Bradman just short. On Monday morning Miller hit Laker for five sixes into the Tavern. The Australians passed 500 and declared. The weather darkened. MCC thirty minutes' batting before lunch. The Australians came into the field chucking the ball hard at each other, broad, tall, sure. Hutton and Robertson took guard against Lindwall and Miller. Robertson caught Tallon off Miller. Lindwall and Miller very fast. The sky black. Edrich caught Tallon off Miller. Last ball before lunch. MCC twenty for two.

After lunch the Australians, arrogant, jocular, muscular, larking down the pavilion steps. They waited, hurling the ball about, eight feet tall. Two shapes behind the pavilion glass. Frozen before emerging a split second. Hutton and Compton. We knew them to be the two greatest English batsmen. Down the steps together, out to the middle. They played. The Australians quieter, wary, tight. Bradman studied them. They stayed together for an hour before Compton was out, and M. P. Donnelly, and Hutton, and the Australians walked home.

First Test at Trent Bridge. The first seven in the English batting order: Hutton, Washbrook, Edrich, Compton, Hard-staff, Barnett, Yardley. They'll never get them out, I said. At lunch on the first day, England seventy-eight for eight.

Hutton.

England versus New Zealand 1949. Hutton opened quietly,

within himself, setting his day in order. At the first hour England forty for none. Hutton looking set for a score. Burtt, slow left hand, took the ball at the Nursery end, tossed it up. To his first ball Hutton played a superb square drive to Wallace at deep point. Wallace stopped it. The crowd leaned in. Burtt again. Hutton flowed into another superb square drive to Wallace's right hand. Wallace stopped it. Back to the bowler. Burtt again, up. Hutton, very hard, a most brilliant square drive to Wallace's left hand. Wallace stopped it. Back to the bowler. The crowd. Burtt in, bowled. Hutton halfway up the pitch immediately, driving straight. Missed it. Clean bowled. On his heel back to the pavilion.

Hutton was never dull. His bat was part of his nervous system. His play was sculptured. His forward defensive stroke was a complete statement. The handle of his bat seemed electric. Always, for me, a sense of his vulnerability, of a very uncommon sensibility. He never just went through the motions, nothing was glibly arrived at. He was never, for me, as some have defined him, simply a 'master technician'. He attended to the particular but rarely lost sight of the context in which it took place. But one day in Sydney he hit thirty-seven in twenty-four minutes and was out last ball before lunch when his bat slipped in hitting a further four, when England had nothing to play for but a hopeless draw, and he's never explained why he did *that*. I wasn't there to see it and probably regret that as much as anything. But I wasn't surprised to hear about it, because every stroke he made surprised me.

I heard about Hutton's thirty-seven on the radio. 7 a.m. Listened to every morning of the 1946/47 series. Alan McGilvray talking. Always England six wickets down and Yardley thirty-five not out. But it was in an Irish kitchen in County Galway that, alone, I heard Edrich and Compton in 1953 clinch the Ashes for England.

Those were the days of Bedser and Wright, Evans, Washbrook and Gimblett, M. P. Donnelly, Smailes and Bowes, A.

[36]

B. Sellars, Voce and Charley Barnett, A. W. Wellard, S. M. Brown and Jim Sims, Mankad, Mustaq Ali, Athol Rowan, even H. T. Bartlett, even Hammond and certainly Bradman.

One morning at drama school I pretended illness and pale and shaky walked into Gower St. Once round the corner I jumped on a bus and ran into Lord's at the Nursery end to see through the terraces Washbrook late cutting for four, the ball skidding towards me. That beautiful evening Compton made seventy.

But it was 1950 when G. H. G. Doggart missed Walcott at slip off Edrich and Walcott went on to score 165, Gomez with him. Christiani was a very good fielder. Ramadhin and Valentine had a good season. Hutton scored 202 not out against them and against Goddard bowling breakbacks on a bad wicket at the Oval.

It was 1949 when Bailey caught Wallace blindingly at silly mid on. And when was it I watched Donnelly score 180 for the Gents versus Players? He went down the afternoon with his lightning pulls.

Constantine hitting a six over fine leg into the pavilion. Talk of a schoolboy called May.

1969

On Being Awarded the German Shakespeare Prize in Hamburg

When I was informed that I was to be given this award my reaction was to be startled, even bewildered, while at the same time to feel deeply gratified by this honour. I remain honoured and slightly bewildered, but also frightened. What frightens me is that I have been asked to speak to you today. If I find writing difficult I find giving a public address doubly so.

Once, many years ago, I found myself engaged uneasily in a public discussion on the theatre. Someone asked me what my work was 'about'. I replied with no thought at all and merely to frustrate this line of enquiry: 'The weasel under the cocktail cabinet.' That was a great mistake. Over the years I have seen that remark quoted in a number of learned columns. It has now seemingly acquired a profound significance, and is seen to be a highly relevant and meaningful observation about my own work. But for me the remark meant precisely nothing. Such are the dangers of speaking in public.

In what way can one talk about one's work? I'm a writer, not a critic. When I use the word work I mean work. I regard myself as nothing more than a working man.

I am moved by the fact that the selection committee for the Shakespeare Prize has judged my work, in the context of this award, as worthy of it, but it's impossible for me to understand the reasons that led them to their decision. I'm at the other end of the telescope. The language used, the opinions given, the approvals and objections engendered by one's work happen in a sense outside one's actual experience of it, since the core of that experience consists in writing the stuff. I have a particular relationship with the words I put down on paper and the characters which emerge from them which no one else can share with me. And perhaps that's why I remain bewildered by praise and really quite indifferent to insult. Praise and insult refer to someone called Pinter. I don't know the man they're talking about. I know the plays, but in a totally different way, in a quite private way.

If I am to talk at all I prefer to talk practically about practical matters, but that's no more than a pious hope, since one invariably slips into theorizing, almost without noticing it. And I distrust theory. In whatever capacity I have worked in the theatre, and apart from writing I have done quite a bit of acting and a certain amount of directing for the stage, I have found that theory, as such, has never been helpful; either to myself, or, I have noticed, to few of my colleagues. The best sort of collaborative working relationship in the theatre, in my view, consists in a kind of stumbling erratic shorthand, through which facts are lost, collided with, fumbled, found again. One excellent director I know has never been known to complete a sentence. He has such instinctive surety and almost subliminal powers of communication that the actors respond to his words before he has said them.

I don't want to imply that I am counselling lack of intelligence as a working aid. On the contrary, I am referring to an intelligence brought to bear on practical and relevant matters, on matters which are active and alive and specific, an intelligence working with others to find the legitimate and therefore compulsory facts and make them concrete for us on the stage. A rehearsal period which consists of philosophical discourse or political treatise does not get the curtain up at eight o'clock.

I have referred to facts, by which I mean theatrical facts. It is true to say that theatrical facts do not easily disclose their secrets, and it is very easy, when they prove stubborn, to distort them, to make them into something else, or to pretend they never existed. This happens more often in the theatre than we care to recognize and is proof either of incompetence or fundamental contempt for the work in hand.

I believe myself that when a writer looks at the blank of the word he has not yet written, or when actors and directors arrive at a given moment on stage, there is only one proper thing that can take place at that moment, and that that thing, that gesture, that word on the page, must alone be found, and once found, scrupulously protected. I think I am talking about necessary shape, both as regards a play and its production.

If there is, as I believe, a necessary, an obligatory shape which a play demands of its writer, then I have never been able to achieve it myself. I have always finished the last draft of a play with a mixture of feelings: relief, disbelief, exhilaration, and a certainty that if I could only wring the play's neck once more it might yield once more to me, that I could get it better, that I could get the better of it, perhaps. But that's impossible. You create the word and in a certain way the word, in finding its own life, stares you out, is obdurate, and more often than not defeats you. You create the characters and they prove to be very tough. They observe you, their writer, warily. It may sound absurd, but I believe I am speaking the truth when I say that I have suffered two kinds of pain through my characters. I have witnessed *their* pain when I am in the act of distorting them, of falsifying them, and I have witnessed their contempt. I have suffered pain when I have been unable to get to the quick of them, when they wilfully elude me, when they withdraw into the shadows. And there's a third and rarer pain. That is when the right word, or the right act jolts them or stills them into their proper life. When that happens the pain is worth having. When that happens I am ready to take them into the nearest bar and buy drinks all round. And I hope they would forgive me my trespasses against them and do the same for me. But there is no question that quite a conflict takes place between the writer and his characters and on the whole I would say the characters are the winners. And that's as it should be, I think. Where a writer sets out a blueprint for his characters, and keeps them rigidly to it, where they do not at any time upset his applecart, where he has mastered them, he has also killed them, or rather terminated their birth, and he has a dead play on his hands.

Sometimes, the director says to me in rehearsal: 'Why does she say this?' I reply: 'Wait a minute, let me look at the text.' I do so, and perhaps I say: 'Doesn't she say this because he said *that*, two pages ago?' Or I say: 'Because that's what she feels.' Or: 'Because she feels something else, and therefore says that.' Or: 'I haven't the faintest idea. But somehow we have to find out.' Sometimes I learn quite a lot from rehearsals.

I have been very fortunate, in my life, in the people I've worked with, and my association with Peter Hall and the Royal Shakespeare Company has, particularly, been greatly satisfying. Peter Hall and I, working together, have found that the image must be pursued with the greatest vigilance, calmly, and once found, must be sharpened, graded, accurately focused and maintained, and that the key word is economy, economy of movement and gesture, of emotion and its expression, both the internal and the external in specific and exact relation to each other, so that there is no wastage and no mess. These are hardly revolutionary conclusions, but I hope no less worthy of restatement for that.

I may appear to be laying too heavy an emphasis on method and technique as opposed to content, but this is not in fact the case. I am not suggesting that the disciplines to which I have been referring be imposed upon the action in terms of a device, or as a formal convenience. What is made evident before us on the stage can clearly only be made fully evident where the content of the scene has been defined. But I do not understand this definition as one arrived at through the intellect, but a definition made by the actors, using quite a different system. In other words, if I now bring various criteria to bear upon a production, these are not intellectual concepts but facts forged through experience of active participation with good actors and, I hope, a living text.

What am I writing about? Not the weasel under the cocktail cabinet.

I am not concerned with making general statements. I am not interested in theatre used simply as a means of self-expression on the part of the people engaged in it. I find in so much group theatre, under the sweat and assault and noise, nothing but valueless generalizations, naïve and quite unfruitful.

I can sum up none of my plays. I can describe none of them, except to say: That is what happened. That is what they said. That is what they did.

I am aware, sometimes, of an insistence in my mind. Images, characters, insisting upon being written. You can pour a drink, make a telephone call or run round the park, and sometimes succeed in suffocating them. You know they're going to make your life hell. But at other times they're unavoidable and you're compelled to try to do them some kind of justice. And while it may be hell, it's certainly for me the best kind of hell to be in.

However, I find it ironic that I have come here to receive this distinguished award as a writer, and that at the moment I am writing nothing and can write nothing. I don't know why. It's a very bad feeling, I know that, but I must say I want more than anything else to fill up a blank page again, and to feel that strange thing happen, birth through fingertips. When you can't write you feel you've been banished from yourself.

1970

On the Screenplay of *A la recherche du temps perdu*

Early in 1972 Nicole Stephane, who owned the film rights to *A la recherche du temps perdu*, asked Joseph Losey if he would like to work on a film version of the book. He asked me if I was interested. We had worked together on three films up to that point: *The Servant*, *Accident* and *The Go-Between*.

I had read only *Du côté de chez Swann*, the first volume of the work, many years before. I expressed great interest in the idea, met Joe and Nicole Stephane and agreed to go ahead. I also proposed that Barbara Bray, who was for many years script editor for BBC Radio and whom I knew to be a Proustian authority, join us in the venture as advisor. Joe and Barbara met and agreed to this.

For three months I read *A la recherche du temps perdu* every day. I took hundreds of notes while reading but was left at the end quite baffled as to how to approach a task of such magnitude. The one thing of which I was certain was that it would be wrong to attempt to make a film centred around one or two volumes, *La Prisonnière* or *Sodome et Gomorrhe*, for example. If the thing was to be done at all, one would have to try to distil the whole work, to incorporate the major themes of the book into an integrated whole. With this Joe and Barbara agreed. We decided that the architecture of the film should be based on two main and contrasting principles: one, a movement, chiefly narrative, towards disillusion, and the other, more intermittent, towards revelation, rising to where time that was lost is found, and fixed for ever in art.

Proust wrote *Du côté de chez Swann* first and *Le Temps retrouvé*, the last volume, second. He then wrote the rest. The relationship between the first volume and the last seemed to us the crucial one. The whole book is, as it were, contained in the last volume. When Marcel, in *Le Temps retrouvé*, says that he is now able to start his work, he has already written it.

We have just read it. Somehow this remarkable conception had to be found again in another form. We knew we could in no sense *rival* the work. But could we be true to it?

It would take much too long now to go into the details of how and why we took the range of decisions, including the sacrifice of characters, revealed in the screenplay. They were dictated by the structure previously decided upon. We evolved a working plan and I plunged in the deep end on the basis of it. The subject was Time. In *Le Temps retrouvé*, Marcel, in his forties, hears the bell of his childhood. His childhood, long forgotten, is suddenly present within him, but his consciousness of himself as a child, his memory of the experience, is more real, more acute than the experience itself. For months I wrote and discussed the results regularly with my colleagues.

In the summer of 1972 we made a number of trips to France; to Illiers, to Cabourg, to Paris, and steeped ourselves in the Proustian locations. In November the screenplay was completed. It was long and clearly very expensive. I cut twenty-four pages, which in fact I thought all to the good, and at the beginning of 1973 the revised version existed and was final.

Working on *A la recherche du temps perdu* was the best working year of my life.

We then all tried to get the money to make the film. Up to this point the film has not been made.

1978

Arthur Wellard

In July 1974 Gaieties CC* was engaged in an excrutiatingly
tense contest with Banstead. We had bowled Banstead out for
175 and had not regarded the task ahead as particularly
daunting. However, we had made a terrible mess of it and
when our ninth wicket fell still needed five runs to win. That
we were so close was entirely due to our opening batsman,
Robert East, who at that point was ninety-six not out. The
light was appalling. Our last man was Arthur Wellard, then
aged seventy-two. He wasn't at all happy about the reigning
state of affairs. He had castigated us throughout the innings
for our wretched performance and now objected strongly to
the fact that he was compelled to bat. I can't see the bloody
wicket from here, how do you expect me to see the bloody
ball? As a rider, his rheumatism was killing him. (He had
bowled eighteen overs for twenty-nine runs in the Banstead
innings.) He lumbered out to the wicket, cursing.

Banstead were never a sentimental crowd. The sight of an
old man taking guard in no way softened their intent. Their
quickie had two balls left to complete the over. He bowled
them, they were pretty quick, and Arthur let both go by
outside the off-stump, his bat raised high. Whether he let
them go, or whether he didn't see them, was a question of
some debate, but something told us that he had seen them,
clearly, and allowed them to pass.

East drove the first ball of the next over straight for four,
bringing up his hundred and leaving us with one run to win.
The next five balls he struck to the deep-set field. There were
clear singles for the asking in these shots but Arthur in each
case declined the invitation, with an uplifted hand. He was

*Gaieties C.C. is a wandering side which plays club cricket in the Home
Counties.

[45]

past the age, his hand asserted, when running singles was anything else but a mug's game.

So Arthur prepared to face what we knew had to be the last over, with one run to win. The Gaieties side, to a man, stood, smoked, walked in circles outside the pavilion, peering out at the pitch through the gloom. It appeared to be night, but we could discern Arthur standing erect, waiting for the ball. The quickie raced in and bowled. We saw Arthur's left leg go down the wicket, the bat sweep, and were suddenly aware that the ball had gone miles, in the long-on area, over the boundary for four. We had won.

In the bar he pronounced himself well pleased. No trouble, he said. He tried to get me with a yorker. Where's the boy who made the ton? He did well. Tell him he can buy me a pint.

Arthur played his last game for Gaieties in 1975. By this time his arm was low and discernibly crooked and his bowling was accompanied by a remarkable range of grunts. He was also, naturally, slow, but his variation of length still asked questions of the batsmen and he could still move one away, late. But he could now be hit and he could no longer see the ball quickly enough to catch it. He retired from the field at the age of seventy-three and became our umpire. He had been playing cricket for some fifty years.

What was Hammond like, Arthur, in his prime? Hammond? I used to bowl against Hammond at Taunton. Jack White set two rings on the off-side, an inner ring and an outer ring. Old Wally banged them through both rings. Off the back foot. Nobody could stop him. Never anyone to touch old Wally on the off-side, off the back foot. What was he like on the front foot, Arthur? He was bloody useful on the front foot, too.

What about Larwood, Arthur? How fast was he? Larwood? He was a bit quick, Larwood. Quickest thing I ever saw. First time I faced him was at Trent Bridge, that was my first season with Somerset. Who's this Larwood? I said, supposed to be a bit pacey, is he? I didn't reckon the stories. He's a bit quick, they said. A bit quick? I said. We'll see about that. I'd faced a few quickies in Kent. Well, I went out there and I got four balls from Larwood and I didn't see any of them. The first I knew about them was Ben Lilley throwing them back. The fifth ball knocked my hob over and I didn't see that one either. I'll tell you, he was a bit quick, Harold Larwood.

Wisden supports this: May 1929. Trent Bridge. Notts v. Somerset. A. W. Wellard b. Larwood 0. What Arthur didn't mention was that in the Notts innings we read: H. Larwood b. Wellard 0.

Did I ever tell you the story about Harry Smith of Leicester? Arthur went on. He had a stutter. One day they went out into the field against Notts. Harry likes the look of the wicket, he thinks it'll suit him. I'll tell you what, S-s-skip, he says to his skipper, I think I'll b-b-bounce one or two. Wait a minute, says the skip, you know who they've got on the other side? They've got Larwood and Voce. I'll just b-b-bounce one or two, says Harry. So he bounces one or two and Notts don't like it much. Anyway, Leicestershire go in before the end of the day and Larwood and Voce knock them over like tin soldiers and suddenly old Harry finds he's at the wicket. Larwood and Voce go for him. Harry's never seen so many balls around his ears. He thinks they're going to kill him. Suddenly he gets a touch and Sam Staples dives at first slip and it looks as though he's caught it. Harry takes off his gloves and walks. Wait a minute, Harry, says Sam, it was a bump ball, I didn't catch it. Yes, you f-f-f-fucking well did, says Harry, and he's back in the pavilion before you can say Jack Robinson.

Arthur would roar at that one but he never missed what was going on in the middle. Even side-on to the pitch and not apparently paying any attention he could see what the ball was doing. She popped, he would say, he wasn't forward enough. It's no good half-arsing about, it's no good playing half-cock on a wicket like this, it's not the bloody Oval. What he wants to do, he wants to get his front foot right forward, see what I mean, get to the pitch of it. Then he stands a chance. The batsman was caught at slip. It was inevitable, said Arthur. Inevitable. He was half-arsing about.

Once, on a beautiful wicket at Eastbourne I suddenly played a cover drive for four, probably the best shot I ever played in my life. A few overs later I was clean bowled. Arthur was waiting for me in front of the pavilion. What do you think you're doing? he asked. What do you mean? I said. What do you think you're doing, playing back to a pitch-up ball? Was it pitched-up? I said. I thought it was short of a length. Short of a length! he exploded. You must be going blind. You made it into a yorker! Oh, I said. Well, anyway, Arthur, what did you think of that cover drive? Never mind the cover drive, Arthur said. Just stop all that playing back to full-length balls. You had a fifty there for the asking. Sorry, Arthur, I said.

Arthur was a stern critic of my batting and with good reason. My skills were limited. There were only two things I could do well. I possessed quite a gritty defence and I could hit straight for six – sometimes, oddly enough, off the back foot. But I didn't do either of these things very often. I had little concentration, patience or, the most important thing of all, true relaxation. And my judgement was distinctly less than impeccable. Listen, son, Arthur would say, you've got a good pair of forearms but just because you give one ball the charge and get away with it doesn't mean you can go out and give the next ball the charge, does it? Be sensible. What do you think the bowler's doing? He's thinking, son, thinking, he's thinking how to get you out. And if he sees you're going to give him the charge every ball he's got you for breakfast. You're supposed to be an intelligent man. Use your intelligence. Sorry, Arthur, I said.

Occasionally I would perform respectably, under Arthur's scrutiny. Once, when we were in terrible trouble, forty for five or something, against Hook and Southborough, I managed to get my head down and stayed at the wicket for an hour and a quarter, for some twenty-five runs; thus, with my partner, warding off disaster. On my return to the pavilion Arthur looked at me steadily and said: I was proud of you. I don't suppose any words said to me have given me greater pleasure.

As is well known, Arthur (until Sobers beat it) held the record for hitting the most sixes in an over; five – off Armstrong of Derbyshire in 1936. He did the same thing in 1938, off Woolley. During his professional career he scored over twelve thousand runs, of which three thousand were in sixes. (He also took over sixteen hundred wickets.) He agreed that he was seeing the ball well against Armstrong and Woolley but the six he remembered above all was one he hit off Amar Singh at Bombay on Lord Tennyson's Indian tour of 1938.

He wasn't a bad bowler, Amar Singh. He moved it about a bit. He dug it in. You had to watch yourself. Anyway, he suddenly let one go, it was well up and swinging. I could see it all the way and I hit it. Well, they've got these stands in Bombay, one on top of the other, and I saw this ball, she was still climbing when she hit the top of the top stand. I was aiming for that river they've got over there. The Ganges. If it hadn't been for that bloody top stand I'd have had it in the Ganges. That wasn't a bad blow, that one.

To do with the same tour, Arthur told us the story about Joe Hardstaff and the Maharajah, the night before the game at Madras. This Maharajah was a big drinker, you see, so he invited a few of us over for a drinking competition one night. Well, I was there and old George Pope and one or two others, but we couldn't take the pace, so we dropped out, round about midnight. Well, this Maharajah, he had everything on the table: whisky, brandy, gin, the lot, and it was left to him and Joe, and Joe had to go with him, glass for glass. Well, Joe went with him, Joe could take a few in those days, and they went at it until five o'clock in the morning and the Maharajah is still standing and Joe suddenly goes out like a light.

Amazing man, that Maharajah, can't remember his name. Anyway, we take Joe home, get him into his bed, he's still not uttering, he's as good as dead, and, my word of honour, we think, Christ, old Joe's gone too far this time. Next day he goes out to bat before lunch, he stays there all day and he makes two hundred. Sweated it all out, you see.

Wisden confirms the innings, at least: Lord Tennyson's Team v. Madras. January 1938. J. Hardstaff c. Gopalan b. Parthasarathi 213. (Hardstaff never appeared in trouble, according to Wisden, and, batting five hours, he hit twenty-four fours.)

As an umpire, Arthur was strictly impartial, by the highest standards, but didn't see the giving of advice to his side as straying from the moral obligations his role imposed. The batsman would grope forward, snick a single through the slips, run, and find Arthur staring at him at the bowler's end. Where's your feet? Arthur would say out of the side of his mouth. You've got feet, haven't you? Use them. You're playing cricket, son, not poker. To our off-break bowler he would mutter: Go round the wicket and bring up another short leg, put him round the corner, give it some air, make the most of it, she's turning, son, she's turning. Or, to me, the captain of the day: What are you doing with a silly mid-off on a wicket like this? Put him out to extra cover. Let the lad have a go. See what I mean? Pretend you're frightened of him. He'll fall for it.

Once, when I was the silly mid-off in question, having declined his advice, I dived and made a catch. As the batsman was retreating, Arthur called me over. Good catch, he said. Except it wasn't a catch. It was a bump ball. Bump ball? I said. It was a clean catch. Cunning bugger, said Arthur. That was a bump ball. The trouble was the man walked. If he'd have stayed where he was and you'd have appealed I'd have given him not out. Anyway, he's out, I said. He's out all right, said Arthur. But I didn't give him out.

He umpired for Gaieties for four years. He never gave a

Gaieties batsman not out when he thought him to be out. Nor did he ever give opposition batsmen out when he considered them to be not out. No chance, he would retort to our lbw appeals, not in the same parish, you must be joking.

Compton and Edrich? On a hiding to nothing, son. Never known anything like it. What year was it, after the war, at Lord's, we got rid of Robertson, we got rid of Brown, and then those two buggers came together and they must have made something like a thousand. I'd been bowling all bloody day and the skipper comes up to me and he says, Go on, Arthur, have one more go. One more go? I said. I haven't got any legs left. One more go, says the skip, go on, Arthur, just one more go. Well, I had one more go and then I dropped dead.

Wisden reports: May 1948. Lord's. Middlesex: Robertson c. Hazell b. Buse 21. Brown c. Mitchell-Innes b. Buse 31. Edrich not out 168. Compton not out 252. Middlesex declared at 478 for 2 fifty minutes before the close of play on the first day. Wellard's analysis: Overs 39. Maidens 4. Runs 158. Wickets 0.

He moved to Eastbourne with his wife in 1977. Once, finding myself in the area, I rang him and arranged to meet him for a drink. I walked into the pub. It was empty, apart from a lone big man, erect at the bar. He was precisely dressed, as always: tweed jacket, shirt and tie, grey flannels, shoes well polished. He passed a glass to me: the glass, like the ball, tiny in his hands. No, he didn't bother much about club cricket in the Eastbourne area. Anyway, his legs were bad. All the old stagers were dropping like flies. Harold Gimblett had topped himself. He was always a nervous kind of man, highly strung. Remember his first knock for Somerset? Made a hundred in just over the hour. He did it with my bat. I lent it to him, you see. He was only a lad.

Yes, he watched a bit of the game on television. Viv Richards was world class. Mind you, Bradman would take a lot of beating, when you came down to it. But Hobbs was probably the best of the lot.

Arthur played for England against Australia at Lord's in 1938. He took two for ninety-six and one for thirty, scored four and thirty-eight (including a six into the Grandstand). He gave me his England cap and the stump he knocked over when he bowled Badcock.

1981

'Jimmy'

In May 1957 my first play, *The Room*, was presented at Bristol University by my old friend, Henry Woolf. Susan Engel, then a student at the university, played the lead.

I was myself a working actor at the time and some months later got a job in a touring farce. One of the dates was Bristol. Money was short. I phoned Susan Engel and she kindly offered me a spare bed in her flat.

We were playing the Bristol Hippodrome. One night after the show I returned to the flat and went straight to bed. About midnight I was awoken by Susan. She told me that John Hall, the author of a play then playing at the Bristol Old Vic, had popped in for a nightcap, bringing with him his literary agent from London. She thought it would be in my interests to meet this agent. I demurred, pleading exhaustion, but she insisted. I put on a dressing gown and went into the kitchen. In the kitchen was Jimmy Wax. He told me he had heard about *The Room* and suggested that Susan and I read a scene from the play. So, at midnight, in Susan's kitchen, in I think July of 1957, I, as it were, auditioned for Jimmy. He laughed a good deal during the reading and asked me to send him the play. The visitors left, Susan was delighted, I went back to bed.

The next week Jimmy wrote proposing that he be my agent. I agreed. When I got back to London we met. I expected to be asked to sign something, but Jimmy said that wasn't necessary. He extended his hand. I took it. We then spoke daily and met weekly for almost twenty-six years.

He was my backbone, through thick and thin.

Jimmy was a man of extraordinarily clear sight. He was straight as a die. He told the truth; not only to me, but, essentially, to theatrical managers and film producers. And most of the time they didn't like it. But he feared no one. He would not be bullied. He was totally independent, a stern and rigorous protector of his author's rights. I think he understood that protection to be in the nature of a moral obligation. (I often referred to him as 'The Reverend' Wax.) He was a wonderful counsellor; his guidance humorous, flexible, critical, wise.

He was a man of truly good cheer, which is not to say that he possessed false optimism or was remotely sentimental. He simply had a sense of perspective, of proportion, which, for all his many passions, allowed him to view life with an affectionate detachment.

I shall never forget his warmth, his kindness, his constancy. He was a rare man, a true friend.

His death is, for me, 'a very limb lopp'd off'.

1984

Samuel Beckett

The farther he goes the more good it does me. I don't want philosophies, tracts, dogmas, creeds, way outs, truths, answers, *nothing from the bargain basement*. He is the most courageous, remorseless writer going and the more he grinds my nose in the shit the more I am grateful to him. He's not fucking me about, he's not leading me up any garden, he's not slipping me any wink, he's not flogging me a remedy or a path or a revelation or a basinful of breadcrumbs, he's not selling me anything I don't want to buy, he doesn't give a bollock whether I buy or not, *he hasn't got his hand over his heart*. Well, I'll buy his goods, hook, line and sinker, because he leaves no stone unturned and no maggot lonely. He brings forth a body of beauty. His work is beautiful.

1954

A WAKE FOR SAM
BBC TV

I first met Samuel Beckett in 1961 in Paris when my play, *The Caretaker*, was being produced. He came into the hotel walking very quickly indeed. He had a sharp stride and quick handshake. He was extremely friendly. I'd known his work for many years of course but it hadn't led me to believe he'd be such a very fast driver. He drove his little Citroën from bar to bar throughout the whole evening, very quickly indeed. We finally ended up in a place in Les Halles eating onion soup at about 4 in the morning and I was by this time overcome – through, I think, alcohol, tobacco and excitement – with indigestion and heartburn, so I lay my head down on the table. When I looked up he was gone. I had no idea where he'd gone and I thought, 'Perhaps this has all been a dream.' I think I went to sleep on the table and about forty-five minutes later the table jolted and there he was and he had a package in his hand, a bag. And he said, 'I've been across the whole of Paris to find this. I finally found it.' And he opened the bag and gave me a tin of bicarbonate of soda, which indeed worked wonders.

1990

A Speech of Thanks

The David Cohen British Literature Prize is awarded
every two years in recognition of a lifetime's achieve-
ment by a living British writer.

This is a great honour. Thank you very much.

I can't say that there was a very strong literary tradition in
my family. My mother enjoyed reading the novels of A. J.
Cronin and Arnold Bennett and my father (who left the
house at 7 a.m. and returned at 7 p.m., working as a jobbing
tailor) liked Westerns but there were very few books about
the house. This was of course also due to the fact that we
depended entirely upon libraries. Nobody could afford to
buy books.

However, when I first had a poem published in a magazine
called *Poetry London* my parents were quite pleased. I
published the poem with my name spelt PINTA, as one of
my aunts was convinced that we came from a distinguished
Portuguese family, the Da Pintas. This has never been con-
firmed, nor do I know whether such a family ever existed.
The whole thing seemed to be in quite violent conflict with
my understanding that all four of my grandparents came
from Odessa, or at least Hungary or perhaps even Poland.

There was tentative speculation that PINTA became
PINTER in the course of flight from the Spanish Inquisition
but whether they had a Spanish Inquisition in Portugal no one
quite seemed to know, at least in Hackney, where we lived.
Anyway I found the PINTA spelling quite attractive, although
I didn't go as far as the 'DA'. And I dropped the whole idea
shortly afterwards.

There was only one member of my family who appeared to
be at all well-off, my great-uncle, Uncle Coleman, who was

'in business'. He always wore felt carpet-slippers and a skull cap at home and was a very courteous man. My father proposed that I show Uncle Coleman my poem in *Poetry London* when we next went to tea. I agreed, with some misgivings. My poem was called 'New Year in the Midlands' (see p. 131) and was to do with a young actor's vagabond life in rep. It was heavily influenced by Dylan Thomas. It contained the following line:

> This is the shine, the powder and blood and here am I,
> Straddled, exile always in one Whitbread Ale town,
> Or such.

My father and I sat in the room in silence, while Uncle Coleman read this poem. When he reached those lines he stopped, looked over the magazine at us and said: 'Whitbread shares are doing very well at the moment. Take my tip.'

That was in 1950, when I was twenty.

My early reading was rather shapeless and disjointed, mainly, I believe, to do with the dislocation of a childhood in wartime. I was evacuated twice (once to Cornwall, where I more or less saw the sea for the first time), went to a number of schools and kept returning to London to more bombs, flying bombs and rockets. It wasn't a very conducive atmosphere for reading. But I finally settled in Hackney Downs Grammar School in late 1944 and made up for lost time. Hackney also had a great Public Library and there I discovered Joyce, Lawrence, Dostoevsky, Hemingway, Virginia Woolf, Rimbaud, Yeats, etc.

Some years later, in I think 1951, having read an extract from Beckett's *Watt* in a magazine called *Irish Writing*, I looked for books by Beckett in library after library – with no success. Eventually I unearthed one – his first novel, *Murphy*. It had been hanging about Bermondsey Public Reserve Library since 1938. I concluded that interest in Beckett was low and decided to keep it – on an extended loan, as it were. I still have it.

In 1944 I met Joseph Brearley, who came to the school to teach English. Joe Brearley was a tall Yorkshireman who suffered from malaria, had been torpedoed at sea in the war and possessed a passionate enthusiasm for English poetry and dramatic literature. There had been no drama in the school when he arrived in 1945 but before we knew where we were he announced that he would do a production of *Macbeth* and, pointing at me in class, said: 'And you, Pinter, will play Macbeth.' 'Me, sir?' I said. 'Yes. You,' he said. I was fifteen and I did play Macbeth, in modern dress, wearing the uniform of a major-general. I was so pleased with this uniform that I wore it on the 38 bus to go home to tea after the dress rehearsal. Old ladies smiled at me. The bus conductor looked at me and said: 'Well, I don't know what to charge you.' My parents gave me the *Collected Plays of Shakespeare* to mark the occasion. I also managed to save up to buy a copy of *Ulysses* which I placed on the bookshelf in the living room. My father told me to take it off the shelf. He said he wouldn't have a book like that in the room where my mother served dinner.

Joe Brearley and I became close friends. We embarked on a series of long walks, which continued for years, starting from Hackney Downs, up to Springfield Park, along the river Lea, back up Lea Bridge Road, past Clapton Pond, through Mare Street to Bethnal Green. Shakespeare dominated our lives at that time (I mean the lives of my friends and me) but the revelation which Joe Brearley brought with him was John Webster. On our walks, we would declare into the wind, at the passing trolley-buses or indeed to the passers-by, nuggets of Webster, such as:

> What would it pleasure me to have my throat cut
> With diamonds? or to be smothered
> With Cassia? or to be shot to death with pearls?
> I know death hath ten thousand several doors
> For men to take their exits: and tis found
> They go on such strange geometric hinges

You may open them both ways: anyway, for heaven's sake,
So I were out of your whispering.

(The Duchess of Malfi)

or:

> O I smell soot,
> Most stinking soot, the chimney's a-fire,
> My liver's purboiled like scotch holly-bread,
> There's a plumber laying pipes in my guts.

(The White Devil)

or:

> My soul, like to a ship in a black storm,
> Is driven I know not whither.

(The White Devil)

or:

> I have caught
> An everlasting cold. I have lost my voice
> Most irrecoverably.

(The White Devil)

or:

> Cover her face; mine eyes dazzle; she died young.

(The Duchess of Malfi)

That language made me dizzy.

Joe Brearley fired my imagination. I can never forget him.

*

I started writing plays in 1957 and in 1958 *The Birthday Party* opened at the Lyric, Hammersmith, was massacred by the critics (with the exception of Harold Hobson) and was taken off after eight performances. I decided to pop in to the Thursday matinée. I was a few minutes late and the curtain had gone up. I ran up the stairs to the dress circle. An usherette stopped me. 'Where are you going?' she said. 'To the dress circle,' I said, 'I'm the author.' Her eyes, as I recall, misted over. 'Oh, are you?' she said. 'Oh, you poor chap.

Listen, the dress circle's closed, but why don't you go in, go in and sit down, darling, if you like, go on.' I went into the empty dress circle and looked down into the stalls. Six people were watching the performance which, I must say, didn't seem to be generating very much electricity. I still have the box office returns for the week. The Thursday matinée brought in two pounds six shillings.

In a career attended by a great deal of dramatic criticism one of the most interesting – and indeed acute – critical questions I've ever heard was when I was introduced to a young woman and her six-year-old son. The woman looked down at her son and said: 'This man is a very good writer.' The little boy looked at me and then at his mother and said: 'Can he do a W?'

I'm well aware that I have been described in some quarters as being 'enigmatic, taciturn, terse, prickly, explosive and forbidding'. Well, I do have my moods like anyone else, I won't deny it. But my writing life, which has gone on for roughly forty-five years and isn't over yet, has been informed by a quite different set of characteristics which have nothing whatsoever to do with those descriptions. Quite simply, my writing life has been one of relish, challenge, excitement. Those words are almost, perhaps, truisms. But in fact they are true. Whether it be a poem, a play or a screenplay – if the relish, challenge and excitement in the language and through that language to character isn't there then nothing's there and nothing can exist.

So while I'm sure I am 'enigmatic, tacitturn, terse, prickly, explosive and forbidding', I've also enjoyed my writing life – and indeed my life – to the hilt and I am deeply gratified to have been awarded this prize.

15 March 1995

Harold Pinter and Michael Billington in Conversation at the National Film Theatre, 26 October 1996

MICHAEL BILLINGTON: *Going back to your school days at Hackney Downs in the 1940s, you supported a Debating Society motion that film is more promising as an art-form than theatre. Would this indicate that film is your first love?*

HAROLD PINTER: No, it means that I knew much more about film than theatre at the time. At the age of fourteen or fifteen I saw many films and very little theatre. I had a very exciting introduction to film. I belonged to a film club and I saw Russian cinema, the French surrealist cinema and German cinema. I also saw the American black and white thrillers and the British war films, of course.

MB: *This was a film club in Hackney itself?*

HP: Yes, it was.

MB: *Obviously you had great expertise because at school you gave a talk on realism and post-realism in French cinema.*

HP: I was passionate about all kinds of cinema. It was a tremendous period – the late thirties and forties – in world cinema, especially for surrealist cinema. I was very taken with Buñuel. I saw *Le Chien andalou* and *L'Age D'or* at a very early age. Buñuel and Salvador Dali left quite extraordinary images in my mind at the time; images that I have never really recovered from. I was very keen on Marcel Carné, *Le Jour se lève*, *Quai des brumes* and so on. So my world was full of the cinema and images. Eisenstein I saw very early, *The Cabinet of Dr Caligari*. It was all there and it was very rich.

MB: *I can detect some affinity between yourself and Buñuel. Buñuel has a passionate scepticism in his films and a refusal to make explicit moral judgements about characters, which seems to me to have left some imprint on you. Do you acknowledge that?*

HP: I think Buñuel was a phenomenon: there was no one like him; nor will there ever be. To say I was influenced by him is to put it much too glibly. He was part of my life. He was a revelation because he was so brutal.

MB: *Was American commercial cinema of the time impressing you just as much? I mean Hitchcock, Hawks, the great American directors.*

HP: No. What appealed to me much more were those very hard films – *Double Indemnity*, and a wonderful film called *The Oxbow Incident*. Then I saw *The Grapes of Wrath*, which left a great impression on me. From the American point of view there was a very hard, realistic substance to those films which moved me very much. There was a film called *Boomerang*, about injustice. The Americans in those days used to make a lot of films about injustice – Spencer Tracey was in many of them and so was Henry Fonda. Henry Fonda made a very beguiling hero.

MB: *One director you didn't mention was Orson Welles. Were you in tune with him?*

HP: Well, of course. Both *Citizen Kane* and *The Magnificent Ambersons* were great films. The thing about the cinema then was that, even though we were at war, it was extraordinarily fresh. I think that because of the circumstances, film-making was under an extraordinary pressure of some sort or another. There's still a certain residue of that left, but very little of that independent spirit which also manages to get the money.

MB: *A substantial area of your work for the cinema are your translations of stage plays to the screen. Recently I showed the Peter Hall film of* The Homecoming *to a group of American students who didn't know the work and they sat there spellbound and shocked by certain moments. Is there a principle you adopt when adapting your own work? In other*

words, not to open it out, but to close it in for the cinema:
not to have extraneous scenes of people in the streets, the
cabs, etc?

HP: In *The Homecoming* I think I had about four shots of
the street which were very good.

MB: *The cab arriving at the front door.*

HP: It's a wonderful cab, yes. And I think you can take
advantage of an external shot. One of my favourite scenes in
The Caretaker was to take the brothers out into the garden.
There was a little pond which was referred to in the text of
the play and I saw the two brothers, played by Robert Shaw
and Alan Bates, standing and simply looking into the pond,
and the old man looking out of the window wondering what
the hell they were doing. But they were simply looking into
the pond in mutual sympathy, in silence. And then, finally, I
remember Alan turned and walked out. That's something
which one can only achieve in the cinema. So I think one can
benefit. I like the adaptations that I have done apart from *The
Birthday Party*, which I did a long time ago, which didn't
really work.

MB: Betrayal *was also a very good film.*

HP: I think it is. In *Betrayal* I had the opportunity to bring in
children, which I think is very important because the act of
adultery and adulterous relationships almost invariably in-
cludes children. In the film of *Betrayal* I was just able to touch
upon the fact that children grow younger under these circum-
stances until they don't exist at all, they're unborn.

MB: *Could we just talk a little bit about your tremendous*
creative partnership with Joseph Losey. How did you first
encounter Losey?

HP: I was invited to write *The Servant* by Michael Anderson
in about 1962. I wrote it but then Michael Anderson couldn't
get the money to make the film, and so Joe Losey, who liked
the script, managed to get enough money to take it on. I met

Joe Losey for the first time and I went round to his house and he said, 'I liked the script.'

I said, 'Oh, thank you.'

And then he said, 'But I don't like this and this and this and this.'

And I said, 'Why not?'

And he said, 'Well, I don't like this for this reason, and this for that reason.'

And so I said, 'Well, why don't you do another movie?' And I left the house. I just said good night. About two days later he called me and said, 'Why don't we try to start again on this matter?'

I said, 'OK', being a man of the utmost goodwill and good humour. I went back and talked about it with Joe and for another twenty-five years we never had a cross word. I never walked out of his house again. It was the happiest professional relationship that I've had in films. It was also remarkable in its consistency. It sustained itself over not merely three films – *The Servant*, *Accident* and *The Go-Between* – but also a fourth, which unfortunately has never been made: *A la recherche du temps perdu*.

MB: *Can you identify what it was about yourself and Losey that allowed you to click – not instantly, but on the second meeting? Was it a shared view of the world, a shared political view, or a shared sense of humour? What were your common themes?*

HP: There was a shorthand which operated between us from the start. I seemed to know what he was going to say before he said it and he seemed to know what I was going to say before I said it. Also I was very aware that he was much more politically precise than I was – concrete for the time – because he had come out of the United States, McCarthy, etc., and I had only been a mere conscientious objector when I was eighteen. He had been cast out of his land, which was a very substantial matter, and I sympathized with that. I also had

[65]

great sympathy with his ideas, which we never needed to discuss at any great length. He had great intuition, and an innate sense of both political and social hierarchies. I knew what he was talking about and I was right with him. In all the films we made together he was very keen to examine how the class structure operated in this country, which never ceased to be a source of amazement to him.

MB: *That element of class features very strongly in the third film you did together,* The Go-Between. *It is about class amongst many other things. What is striking about the film is how technically risky and adventurous it is, because it seems that you eliminate any hard and fast dialogue between past and present in the finished film. It begins with the aged Leo going back. We only gradually find out who he is. We flash backwards and forwards in time constantly. Did this present problems when it came to showing the film to the front office, as it were?*

HP: Yes, it did indeed. In those days, however, the writer and director both together had an extraordinary strength. In *The Go-Between*, there are essentially flash-forwards of Michael Redgrave, sixty years later. The boy becoming a very elderly man and suddenly appearing out of a car and so on. And as you say, gradually, the identification between the man and the boy and the boy who is to become the old man becomes clearer. But front office said, 'Oh, for Jesus' sake, you can't do this. No one's going to understand what the hell is going on here.' So Joe and I said, 'Yes, they will and it's staying exactly as it is.' Now this is rather extraordinary because in these days the writer and director could say, 'It stays exactly as it is' and nobody will take a blind bit of notice. The whole thing will be recut and re-edited before you know where you are. Very few directors have real control over the final cut, but we felt the courage of our convictions.

MB: *And that was partly because of your solidarity as a team?*

HP: Absolutely. If either of us had flinched, then we'd have been doomed. But the great thing about Joe was that he was so adventurous himself. He was always looking to expand the frontiers of cinema. Unfortunately on the whole he had a terribly tough time trying to get people to believe in what he was doing. But for me making those films with him was a great experience. It's like they happened yesterday.

MB: *And they're still part of the cinema consciousness because they're shown very frequently. They're part of our memories. One thing intrigues me: with each of these three films you got more experimental in the handling of time; time became more fluid. I wonder did that have any effect, do you think, on your writing for the theatre? Because it is very interesting that shortly after* The Go-Between *you wrote* Old Times *for the theatre, and that play again uses time with much greater freedom and flexibility than your early work. Do you think your cinema work was gradually permeating your work for the theatre?*

HP: I have to say I've never sat back outside or up there and looked down on my work one way or the other and been able to make any kind of judgement, and I've certainly never made any correspondence between my work in the cinema and my work in the theatre; it just echoed a natural progression in my life. But evidently, I would have thought that both things affected each other in my sensibility, my artistic sensibility. Must have done. But I can't make any real pronouncements about it. It's not possible.

MB: *Your first non-stage film was of* The Servant, *which was adapted from a novella by Robin Maugham. The Robin Maugham story is a first-person narrative, it's a story set just after the Second World War and it almost seems to be a parable about the class revolution that many people feared might take place under a Labour government. When you adapted it, it underwent a sea change in terms of setting, implication, etc. Was this your decision? Or was it a joint decision? How did the adaptation happen?*

HP: Well, firstly, I still like this film very much indeed, but I did write it thirty-six years ago and I can't say that I had any structure – in other words, political, social or critical – in mind. I was simply working from the images in the story – that's the way I work most often.

MB: *But you made some fairly radical changes; first of all you dropped first-person narration.*

HP: I've only had one piece of first-person narration in anything I've ever written and that's my Proust screenplay which has never been filmed, and that was the last line. One line of first-person narration.

MB: *What is the technical argument against first-person narration in cinema?*

HP: One thing I don't like about French cinema as it developed was what seemed to me to be a very self-conscious commentary on the images and what we were actually seeing – on the tale being told. I became extremely irritated by, for example, seeing a young woman on-screen with perspiration on her brow and her voice-over saying, 'Oh, I was so hot that day.' I think most first-person narrative which illustrates what you're actually looking at is redundant. I believe that a film should tell the tale through images. I'm not talking about voice-over, which is another thing altogether, and the movement between the voice, the mind, the memory and the image – that's clearly another state of affairs.

MB: *So that's what made you change it. But there is a major shift in period because it is post-1945, just after the war, and it seems very much to me to be about the fear of this new class that may arise and destroy the old master's servant. Why did you shift it?*

HP: I really don't know why I shifted it. I can only say now, at this distance, that it was to do with the death of a set of assumptions, on the part of the master. He was part of a tradition which assumed that everything would be the same: there would always be a benevolence there from the servant to the master; there would always be a kitchen available for him, there would always be money and there would always be this kind of influence where you can't go wrong. What we were actually looking at in *The Servant* was that the master was a dying specimen and the servant was taking full advantage of that and good luck to him.

MB: *For me the impact in the Maugham novella is the exact opposite: it's a sigh of regret that this master-class is dying.*
HP: Well, I don't share that view.

MB: *In general terms what is the responsibility of the screenwriter to his or her source? If you're asked to make a screenplay out of a novel, do you have any obligations to the novelist?*
HP: Yes, absolutely. When I say I didn't share that view I meant that nevertheless I regard what I did as being faithful to the actual story. I simply told the story but it emerged with a slightly different perspective. It's also a lot to do with your own interpretation. Other people could take the author's original interpretation but I want to make it absolutely clear that the only point of doing a screenplay of a novel is to be faithful to the intentions of the book as I understand it.

MB: *The second film you did with Losey was* Accident, *and it seems to me that one of the fascinations with that film is the relationship with Nicholas Mosley's original book. Again, you've dropped first-person narration. In the book it's all told by Stephen, the philosophy don. There are two basic narrative changes in your screenplay. One is that the don, played by Dirk Bogarde, makes love to Anna – indeed, implicitly rapes her. You also cut a crucial scene in the book where Stephen, the don, discusses with Charlie, the Stanley Baker character, the whole business of perjuring themselves to protect this woman, Anna. Now, can you explain the rationale behind those changes?*

HP: Firstly, the sexual encounter, the rape, as you say, which it more or less is. I just felt it was a logical progression from two points of view. One is the emotion which is unleashed in the light of the accident; and the second in relation to power. I felt that Dirk Bogarde, Stephen, chose to exercise the power which he actually possessed at that moment. I wrote to Nicholas Mosley about this and I was well aware that it was a big change. I said, 'Look, this is what I've done and you may not agree, but I feel that it possesses integrity, if you like.' And he saw it. Not entirely, but he could see the logic of it, that's all. The second scene about the discussion of the perjury seemed to me much too discursive and I thought it had no place; it was much too self-conscious.

MB: *The relationship between the screenplay and the source is interesting. You are impelled to do an adaptation because you believe in the book and the story, but at the same time, as the adaptor, the story becomes yours.*

HP: Well, I think that's inevitable. But as long as you are expressing the nut of the whole thing – the core of it – I do believe you're keeping faith with it. If you respect it – and there's no other way of writing a screenplay adaptation of a novel – then you can't do it down, you can't be false to it. Maybe there are one or two authors who don't think that. I do remember one film, *Turtle Diary*, which I don't think was successful, and the author, Russell Hoban, positively hated it. I was very upset by that but I understood why he did. We didn't bring it off, simple as that. He didn't think we had found the inner world and he was right. Whereas the relationship between Paul Schrader and me in *The Comfort of Strangers* was good because he understood exactly what was intended and knew how to express it. So if I'm not directing the film but have a good relationship with the director, I'm a happy man really.

The bulk of my screenplays have been shot without any change in them. I worked it out: twenty-two screenplays, two of which have not been filmed – that's the Proust and *Victory*. Out of the twenty left, seventeen have been shot as written and I must say I am rather proud of that. I remember when I saw *The Quiller Memorandum* when it was in the final cut, there was something I had missed. There was a shot where George Segal was driving a sports car and in the mirror he saw a big Mercedes coming up beside him. Segal had been drugged. His car stopped at the traffic lights. The driver of the Mercedes got out and opened Segal's door. I had written, 'I'll drive, move over,' and the actor had said, 'Move over, I'll drive.' I couldn't believe it. I nearly said, 'Stop. How dare you!' because I knew that wasn't what I had written.

MB: *How often do you consult the author himself?*
HP: I do occasionally. With *The French Lieutenant's Woman* I had one or two chats with John Fowles. I said, 'Look, you've written a happy scene here in the book and I simply can't write a happy scene. Why don't you have a go?' I can write happy scenes, I do my best to do so all the time, but in this particular context I was unable to do it. It was a proposal of marriage and I couldn't get the hang of it and John Fowles said, 'What about this, that and the other,' and I said, 'Yes, I see, of course...' You know, cinema is all about collaboration.

Writing, Politics and *Ashes to Ashes*

An interview with Harold Pinter by Mireia Aragay and Ramon Simó, Universitat de Barcelona, Departement de Filologia Anglesa i Alemanya, 6 December 1996

MIREIA ARAGAY: *What does writing mean for you?*

HAROLD PINTER: I was always extremely excited by language from a very early age. I started writing when I was eleven or twelve. I loved words as a child, and that excitement has remained with me all my life. I still feel as excited now as I ever did about words on a page and about the blank piece of paper and the words that might fill it. Every piece of blank paper is an unknown world which you're going to dive into. That is very challenging.

MA: *In 1961, in a conversation with Richard Findlater which was subsequently published as 'Writing for Myself', you stated that 'I start off with people, who come into a particular situation. I certainly don't write from any kind of abstract idea.' Has your creative process remained the same over the years?*

HP: Yes, I've never written from an abstract idea at all. It isn't so much necessarily specific characters as specific and concrete images, either visual or verbal.

MA: *Even in your more recent political plays, is that the way you go about writing?*

HP: Yes, even in my more recent *overtly* political plays. If you're going to write a play about these states of affairs, you've got to have an impulse, and the impulse must come from a specific image. For example, *One for the Road*, which I think has been given a splendid production at the Sala Beckett, began in my mind with a man sitting at a desk waiting for someone to come into the room, his victim. The image of the man sitting at the desk was the concrete fact that started the play. It wasn't the idea that started the play, it was the image of the man that got it going.

RAMON SIMÓ: *When discussing your creative process, you never mention planning or preconceived structures, yet your plays are formally extremely precise. Could you comment on how these two aspects co-exist in your work?*

HP: The formal construction is in the course of the work on the play. I still find that I have to construct very precise forms; it's part of the way I was born. I have the impulse, and then I have to organize that impulse and make it coherent. That coherence is to do with how you shape the language and the structure of the play, quite obviously. I take a great deal of care to do that. So the two things coincide; one is part of the other. I've got an animal in the middle of the play which has to be held by the author. But I like the animal, by the way. If it wasn't for the animal, there'd be nothing there at all.

MA: *How do you try to solve the aesthetic and ethical difficulties inherent in the writing of political plays? How do you avoid preaching to the audience, becoming a kind of prophet?*

HP: It *is* a great trap in writing political plays as such if you know the end before you've written the beginning. I have tried to avoid that and find it afresh, and I hope I'm not sermonizing. I like to find what the state of affairs is and just let it happen. *Party Time* is a case in point. I started with the idea of a party in a very elegant and wealthy apartment in a town somewhere. It became clear as I was writing it that outside in the streets something else was happening. Gradually it became even clearer that what was happening in the streets, which was an act of repression, had actually been organized by the people in this room. But the people in the room naturally never discussed it, just one or two fleeting references. They were drinking champagne and eating canapés and they were very, very happy. They knew that it was all going well. In other words, there was a world which didn't actually bother to discuss the acts of military and police repression for which they were responsible. This emerged during the course of the play. I was quite excited by that, in that it never became really very explicit, but it was as clear as a bell, I think. Without making any great claims, I believe it's an image that has a universal reference. I believe that there *are* extremely powerful people in apartments in capital cities in all countries who are actually controlling events that are happening on the street in a number of very subtle and sometimes not so subtle ways. But they don't really bother to talk about it, because they know it's happening and they know they have the power. It's a question of how power operates.

RS: *The general feeling across Europe now, among play-wrights and people involved in the theatre generally, is that political theatre is quite an impossibility.*

HP: Political theatre now is even more important than it ever was, if by political theatre you mean plays which deal with the real world, not with a manufactured or fantasy world. We are in a terrible dip at the moment, a kind of abyss, because the assumption is that politics are all over. That's what the propaganda says. But I don't believe the propaganda. I believe that politics, our political consciousness and our political intelligence are not all over, because if they are, we are really doomed. I can't myself live like this. I've been told so often that I live in a free country, I'm damn well going to be free. By which I mean I'm going to retain my independence of mind and spirit, and I think that's what is obligatory upon all of us. Most political systems talk in such vague language, and it's our responsibility and our duty as citizens of our various countries to exercise acts of critical scrutiny upon that use of language. Of course, this means that one does tend to become rather unpopular. But to hell with that.

RS: *Brutality and the obvious are always present in your political plays. Aren't these two elements limiting when it comes to discussing politics?*

HP: My plays are not political discussions. They are living things. They are certainly not debates. They *are* violent. Violence has always been in my plays, from the very beginning. *The Room* ends with a sudden, totally gratuitous act of violence on the part of a man who kicks a negro to death. I was quite young at the time, but looking back it doesn't seem to me to be a wild or bizarre thing. We are brought up every day of our lives in this world of violence.

RS: *What's the aim of building such brutal, obvious images in your political plays?*
HP: There's no aim. I do not have an ideology in my plays. I just write; I'm a very instinctive writer. I don't have a calculated aim or ambition; I simply find myself writing something which then follows its own path. And that path tends to include acts of violence of one kind or another, because it is the world in which I live. And so do you.

MA: *Brutality and violence are often related to the male characters in your plays, whereas the women, especially in the plays you wrote in the 1960s, are enigmatic, mysterious, they have a kind of staying power which the men don't seem to have.*
HP: They also tend in later plays to be victims of male brutality.

MA: *Don't you think those are rather stereotypical views of men and women?*
HP: Possibly.

MA: *Do you stand by them?*
HP: I think that men are more brutal than women, actually. There's a terrible two-line poem by Kingsley Amis, in which he says: 'Women are so much nicer than men / No wonder we like them.' My wife considers these lines to be very patronizing and they certainly are, I quite agree. But nevertheless I just believe that God was in much better trim when He created woman. Which doesn't mean to say I sentimentalize

[75]

women. I think women are very tough. But if you look at what has happened in the world since day one, the actual acts of brutality have been dictated by men. Sometimes they have been exercised by women, that is certainly true. In the German camps the women did fine from that point of view; they really fulfilled what was asked of them as men, or rather it didn't matter; they were hardly women, they weren't men, they were just people acting for their state, for their God. Nevertheless in my plays women have always come out in one way or another as the people I feel something towards which I don't feel towards men.

MA: *That's a very male point of view, isn't it?*
HP: Why not?

MA: *There is a lot of violence in your plays, but there is also a great deal of humour, as you reminded us last night at the Sala Beckett. What is the role of humour in your plays? How does it function? Why is it there, in the middle of the brutality?*
HP: Humour is such a mysterious thing, I can't really answer the question. Humour is part of my own upbringing. I don't write what I call funny things, but some of them do make me laugh. I find myself laughing while I'm writing and I notice one or two people also laugh, occasionally.

MA: *I was surprised on the opening night of* Ashes to Ashes *in Barcelona to hear the audience laughing. When I read the play it didn't seem to me to be dealing with anything particularly funny.*
HP: Yes, there *are* some laughs in *Ashes to Ashes*. But I think they stop. The comic, in a way, is the best of what we are. I don't think I write very cruel funny things; I think I write quite affectionate humour, although it can be pretty terse and critical. But on the whole, the laughter goes out of any play I've written before it's finished. I can't think of any play of mine in which there are really any laughs at all in the last ten minutes. But it's not calculated; it's instinctive.

RS: *Last night at the Sala Beckett, the audience laughed during the performance of* One for the Road. *Do you think that is an adequate reception of the play?*

HP: That depends. I'd be very surprised to hear that they laughed in the scene between Nicolas and Gila. But there *are* other laughs. We also laugh when we recognize the ugliness of people, the ugliness in ourselves. It's very much a question of recognition of our own worst characteristics. So I've actually contradicted myself. I've said laughter is created by true affection; it's also created by quite the opposite, by a recognition of where we are ugly.

MA: *According to Simon Gray, in* One for the Road *you are also on the side of Nicolas somehow. Now you said many years ago, in relation to* The Birthday Party *and* The Homecoming, *that you didn't love or hate any of your characters more than any other. Would you make the same point in relation to your political plays, such as* One for the Road?

HP: I'm not terribly fond of Nicolas; I could do without him. Nevertheless, I recognize the plight he's in. Don't forget Nicolas is a deluded man; he's a man possessed, religiously really. He's enacting a religious and political obsession, and I feel very sorry for him. He's an absolute disaster, but the society he's speaking for is in itself a disaster. Coming back to that old cliché – but it's a cliché based on absolute evidence – he will go home to his wife and children, and listen to music, as is touched upon in the production at the Sala Beckett – the music, absolutely right. That the torturers listen to music and are very kind to their children has been well established throughout twentieth-century history. This is one of the very complex states of affairs in the psychology of our social and political lives. I have no answer to any of these; I'm just tapping.

RS: *In 'Writing for the Theatre', the speech you delivered in 1962 before the National Student Drama Festival held at Bristol, you defended the self-sufficiency of art by claiming* that 'What I write has no obligation other than to itself.' Do you still hold that view or has it been modified in any way?

HP: I still essentially feel the same as I did then. I feel that my first obligation is to the work in hand. What I was really talking about when I said that was that I don't feel I have any obligation or responsibility to my public. The public will always do whatever it does. But I have a responsibility towards the text. For example, *Old Times* and *Betrayal*, which are the basis of a rather brilliant construction by the group from Argentina, are not in any sense political plays; they've no political life, they're about other things. But I feel the same responsibility to those plays as I do to my more political plays. So my first responsibility, whatever the nature of the play, is always to the play itself. What I mean is I won't be budged; I won't ever change a play once it's written.

MA: *Is that the reason why over the years you have come to direct several of your own plays? Do you think the playwright is the only legitimate interpreter of his or her own plays?*

HP: No. I really enjoy seeing what other directors do with my plays.

MA: *What do you think is the duty of a director towards the text he or she is directing?*

HP: In Barcelona I've seen three productions of my plays, *One for the Road*, *A Slight Ache* and then two productions in one of *Betrayal* and *Old Times*. What I enjoyed in all of them was the relish which not only the director but also the actors embodied. I think theatre is about relish, passion, engagement. It also leads to adventure. It's not a careful activity, it's a very dangerous activity. But danger can happen in many ways. For example, my production of *Ashes to Ashes* was a very quiet one. People were very still and hardly raised their voice. There are many ways of expressing this perilous fact of life which theatre is all about.

[78]

MA: *As a director, you're often described as very meticulous, and yet you speak of the danger.*

HP: It's the same thing as I was asked about my writing plays; I hope I'm both spontaneous and meticulous, you can be both things at the same time. There's a line in *Party Time* about death being both quick and slow at the same time; I think directing plays can be quick and slow at the same time. The whole point about directing plays and engaging with plays – I'm sure every actor here will know this out of their own discoveries – is that you don't know where you're going, but you've got to find out, and then when you find out you don't know what the next step is going to be either. But it's very important not to collapse on the stage and say, 'I don't know where I'm going'; you've got to keep your feet, but it's very precarious.

MA: *You do enjoy acting, don't you?*

HP: I've been an actor all my life. I started in school when I was sixteen. Then I became a professional actor when I was nineteen. I was very very fortunate because I was plunged into a world of Shakespeare in Ireland with the great actor-manager Anew McMaster and I played in *Hamlet, Othello, Oedipus Rex, Julius Caesar, King Lear*, one night after the other. We played several nights a week in Irish villages. I was twenty at the time and I could take it. It was a very rich existence, and I was introduced into this whole Shakespearian world too, which was wonderful.

RS: *How should actors deal with your plays? When they ask you about the underlying motivations of your characters, you often answer, 'Just do it'.*

HP: Alan Ayckbourn tells this story which I don't really believe is true. I directed him in *The Birthday Party* when he was an actor in 1959. He did say to me, when I first met him, 'Can you tell me where this character comes from, where he lived, who his parents were?' I just said, 'Mind your own business. Just do it.' But I don't really believe I said that, because there are perfectly legitimate questions for an actor to ask. The trouble is I can't answer all that many of them. I literally do not know what some of my characters were doing the day before yesterday. I've always felt, and that's what makes writing very exciting for me, that I meet these characters having not known them before. I don't plan them at all, I don't write any literature about them to myself; I just find them, and therefore I have to find out about them.

MA: *Could you tell us what prompted you to write* Ashes to Ashes?

HP: *Ashes to Ashes* is about two characters, a man and a woman, Devlin and Rebecca. From my point of view, the woman is simply haunted by the world that she's been born into, by all the atrocities that have happened. In fact they seem to have become part of her own experience, although in my view she hasn't actually experienced them herself. That's the whole point of the play. I have myself been haunted by these images for many years, and I'm sure I'm not alone in that. I was brought up in the Second World War. I was about fifteen when the war ended; I could listen and hear and add two and two, so these images of horror and man's inhumanity to man were very strong in my mind as a young man. They've been with me all my life, really. You can't avoid them, because they're around you simply all the time. That is the point about *Ashes to Ashes*. I think Rebecca inhabits that.

MA: *The obvious question is, is it a play about Nazism?*

HP: No, I don't think so at all. It *is* about the images of Nazi Germany; I don't think anyone can ever get that out of their mind. The Holocaust is probably the worst thing that ever happened, because it was so calculated, deliberate and precise, and so fully documented by the people who actually did it. Their view of it is very significant. They counted how many people they were murdering every day, and they looked upon it, I take it, like a car delivery service. How many cars can you make in one day, how many people can you kill in one day?

And there's the whole question of how many people knew what. In the recently published *Hitler's Willing Executioners*, Daniel Goldhagen claims that the majority of the German public was well aware of what was happening. It's certainly true, for example, that in the early days when they were killing people by gas in trucks, the engineers had to work out a way to do it which was practical and effective. These trucks weren't doing very well because they were lopsided, so that when the gas started to go in people would rush to the back of the truck, which could fall over. They had to readjust the structure of the truck so that people would be killed without bothering the driver. This firm of engineers is still going very strong today; it's actually a great car empire in Germany. This also applied to many other people, like the people who made the gas. They weren't making it for killing chickens. But it's not simply the Nazis that I'm talking about in *Ashes to Ashes*, because it would be a dereliction on my part to simply concentrate on the Nazis and leave it at that. Again, as I try to say in the article I published in the *Guardian* on Wednesday (see p. 231), it's not simply that the United States, in my view, has created the most appalling state of affairs all over the world for many years, it's also that what we call our democracies have subscribed to these repressive, cynical and indifferent acts of murder. We sell arms to all the relevant countries, do we not? Not just the United States, but also Great Britain, France, Germany *and* Spain are very active in this field. And they still pat themselves on the back and call themselves a democracy. I wonder what the term 'democracy' actually means. If you are a democracy and you help people of other countries murder their own citizens, then what are you doing? What is that? What *is* that? What does it mean? I don't really understand how the United States can be regarded and regard itself as a democracy just on the basis that it has elections every five years, if it also keeps 1.5 million people in prison and also possesses, the most barbaric of all things, the death penalty in thirty-eight states out of fifty. The death penalty has been abolished more or less all over the world, while our most enlightened democracy, the leader of what is usually called the free world, kills people in thirty-eight states, including young people under eighteen and mentally deficient people, by gassing them, electrifying them, by lethal injection. Or take England; in England now the general political philosophy is to punish and to attribute blame and guilt to the innocent victim. One of the guilty elements in our society is the unmarried mother or single parent, and there are many of them. They are in the main dispossessed and alone, helpless and bewildered, treated by men casually and with no regard for their welfare. *They are treated with equal disregard by the state.* The single mother becomes a guilty person and welfare is taken away from her. We have many more beggars on the streets now than we've had in years, and many of them are single mothers with babies. I don't call that particularly democratic. The word democracy begins to stink. These things, as you can see, are on my mind. So in *Ashes to Ashes* I'm not simply talking about the Nazis; I'm talking about us and our conception of our past and our history, and what it does to us in the present.

MA: *Both the audience's and the critics' reception of* Ashes to Ashes *was much warmer here than it had been in London. The actors and yourself said you were much more pleased with the audience's reaction here than in Britain. What was the difference?*

HP: I'm very glad you ask me that question, because there *was* a very pronounced difference. What we appreciated here was the fullness of the response, the intelligence, and more than that the willingness to enter into the play, to be part of it. The world we've been encouraged to inhabit in London is a world of cynicism and indifference, so many people – there were of course people who did listen, and did the same thing as happened in Barcelona, but they were really a minority – simply refused to listen, and what they did was cough.

MA: *What about the critics?*

HP: The critics didn't cough, I think. In London, both publicly and critically, it was a much more spasmodic experience. In Barcelona it was a much fuller experience, and I was very happy to be here.

MA: *English critics and the English press have generally been rather hostile to your work in recent years, especially after you became publicly involved in political affairs. How do you account for that? How does it relate to the state of Britain in the last few years?*

HP: In Britain there is no tradition of artists being respected; artists are actually *not* respected. Nor is there a tradition of artists being in any way engaged in politics, as there is on the Continent. There's also a very deep-seated tradition of mockery; mockery is the one thing they can still keep going. It comes easily for the English people to mock. It's a very odd situation indeed in England; you try to address real facts of life that surround you and are treated with great hostility.

MA: *When you organized the June 20 Group, with your wife and other writers and intellectuals, you were indeed treated with great animosity.*

HP: We started the group simply to question the appalling situation we found ourselves in in England under Mrs Thatcher's regime, which was destroying so many institutions and convictions that we thought were really part of the essence of England. We were being given another thing altogether, which was that the essence of England was, as I said, punishment, and making money. Mrs Thatcher, I remind you, said immortally: 'There is no such thing as society.' One of her really great statements. And she meant it. She meant by it that we have no obligation or responsibility to anyone else other than ourselves. This has encouraged the most appalling greed and corruption in my society. For example, recently electricity has been privatized in a number of different constructs, procedures and bodies. The

[83]

people who found themselves owning the electricity companies sold them to somebody else for 27 million pounds. These twelve directors walked away with 27 million pounds, whereas old-age pensioners and the poor, of whom there are more and more and more, can hardly pay the electricity bill. That, I find, is an extraordinarily blatant and corrupt use of power; it's totally cynical. In the 1980s, through the June 20 Group, we were drawing attention to this kind of thing in no uncertain terms, but we were undermined finally by the hostility generally surrounding us, and the thing collapsed.

MA: *Was it a form of censorship, in a way, on the part of the media?*

HP: It *is* a brilliant form of censorship, but then it's not actually censorship, it's just derision. If you have derision day after day after day, you think, I give up. But that was a weak moment on our part, certainly on *my* part. I no longer feel that way. I feel no sense of giving up, and I believe there are many people in my country who feel the same thing. The only trouble is that we have an opposition, the new Labour Party, as it calls itself, which desperately wants to become the government. This is almost certainly going to happen, because people have been nauseated by the Conservative government over the last seventeen years. But in the meantime the Labour Party has allowed very bad bills to become law without any protest whatsoever because they simply don't want to rock the boat. This is an absolute disgrace, in my view. For example, the Police Bill is going through Parliament at this moment. It will legalize police bugging of private houses. MI5, the secret service, has this provision too, but they have to go to the Home Secretary for permission. But the police need only go to the Chief Constable and say, 'We're going to do this to him, him, him, her, her, her.' And the general application will by no means be restricted to terrorists or criminals; it will actually apply to people who go on strike, people who write letters to the papers, like me, and all dissenting voices. In other words, it means that the police can do exactly what they like. I think that this is an appallingly undemocratic law, but it has been agreed by the opposition. The Prevention of Terrorism Act has recently come to the same thing. There's a big IRA problem and has been over the years, there's no question about that. But nevertheless, this Prevention of Terrorism Act means that anyone could be stopped on the street for no reason at all, simply at a policeman's whim. He will simply ask the person to show him his wallet or open her handbag. If the person refuses, she's under arrest, and can be given six months in prison. On Monday morning, when I get back from here, I'm going to the trial of a friend of mine who was one of forty-one people who simply sat down a couple of months ago outside an arms trade conference in London as a peaceful protest, doing no harm at all, but simply registering their disapproval. They were all arrested. I believe this kind of thing masquerades under the terms democracy and freedom. I'm not saying that Britain is a totalitarian country. I'm saying, however, that there are totalitarian measures which countries which call themselves democracies can easily employ. The British Parliament was once called, by a Conservative in fact, an 'elected dictatorship'.

MA: *You're saying that there's no opposition left in Britain; is there any Left left in Britain, or in Europe?*
HP: There's a little bit of Left left in Britain. I pray that there is a Left left in Europe, but we have to recognize that the forces against the Left are very great and very ruthless. By the Left I also mean, incidentally, the poor. It seems to me the poor have become the real enemy of the rich. They always have been, but now it's being embodied in concrete terms. Now the communists are no longer in operation as a world-wide force, the poor have become the new force of subversion, because they do affect the stability of the state. So the only thing to do with the poor is keep them poor. I believe this

[85]

operates very strongly. Nicaragua, which I was very, very close to in the 1980s, is a case in point. The Sandinista Revolution, in my opinion and my observation, was a really serious, responsible, intelligent, thoughtful and concerned action. It was inevitable, it happened; and what they then did was to cultivate and establish social systems in Nicaragua which had never been seen before. I'm talking about health and education, literacy, doing away with disease; actually bringing people back from the dead, giving them life. People who'd been totally poverty-stricken all their lives. This was a really responsible act, which was then totally destroyed by the United States. And this has gone under the blanket. It's as if it never happened, but it *did* happen. And one has to keep drawing attention. I find what the Sandinista Revolution was doing was really valuable, important, and *civilized*. If I sound possibly very pronounced in my views about the United States, some might say over the top, I believe that what I'm saying is based on actual facts and actual states of affairs.

MA: *What is your relationship with your own Jewish identity?*

HP: I was never a religious Jew. The last religious subscription I made, the bar mitzvah, was when I was thirteen, which is a long time ago now. That's the last time I was in a synagogue, apart from one or two weddings and one or two funerals. I've no religious beliefs whatsoever, but I'm still Jewish. I don't know what that means, really, nobody ever does. But what I know it does not mean is that I subscribe to what is happening in the state of Israel. I deplore what is happening in Israel, and I've made my position very clear. Not as a Jew, but as a citizen, as a man. For example, I'm a trustee of the Vanunu estate; he's been in prison for over nine years now in solitary confinement and he has another nine to go, for simply reporting on the Israeli nuclear capability. I've been to the Israeli embassy in London many times in this

[86]

connection. When my mother was alive, she certainly didn't like that at all. But of course my mother and father belong to a different generation; I understand why they felt so strongly that you couldn't criticize Israel, because they were brought up in the 1920s and 1930s. But I'm not in that position. Again something that's happening under cover is the detention camps that still exist in the West Bank, in the Sinai desert. Many Palestinians are still in prison in detention camps, many of them without charge at all. I think this is really appalling, and I think the last election in Israel was a disaster. I believe there may be real civil unrest over there because it's really a fifty-fifty thing.

RS: *In your* Guardian *article you also talk about memory, about the way it is manipulated by power, by the media. How can the ordinary person fight this process and not be engulfed by it?*

HP: That is precisely the point, indeed. The terrible thing is that the media is now used politically all over the world. There is such a relationship between the media and the people in political power that it's very difficult to see any distinction between one and the other. This is certainly the case when you look at television. Television all over the world now is more or less run by about three people, as far as I can gather. You switch on any given news programme and see precisely the same thing in the Sahara desert as you do here and in London, because there is a central control. In other words, that news is highly selective and very specifically controlled news coming from somewhere ... the words Rupert Murdoch are not far from my lips, I have to say. But it's not just Rupert Murdoch. In England now, our opposition, which might very well become the next government, has made great friends with Rupert Murdoch. They've done that because he's got a kind of power that they want to lock into. That's a very corrupt state of affairs. It all comes down to power is money and money is power. That's a cliché which you know as well as I do, but it nevertheless does remain the case in so many really repulsive ways. What I find very dispiriting is how the controls that are in place all over the world have really undermined people to a terrible extent, for very practical reasons. Only recently, in England, I was talking to some people about this kind of thing; it was very much a university audience. A man got up and said, 'Now look, I agree with what you're saying, but I'm a lecturer at Cardiff University, and I could not possibly say this myself publicly.' Somebody else said, 'But you're not saying you'd lose your job?' And he said, 'No, I don't think I'd lose my job, but I would not be promoted.' This is an extraordinary and very horrifying curb on free speech, in what we call a democracy, by the way. You asked what can the man in the street do. I think what we can do, since we're all men and women of the street, is simply keep it right there (*touches his forehead*) and try to articulate it.

[11]

Kullus

I

I let him in by the back door.
There was a brisk moon.
  —Come in.
He stepped inside, slapping his hands, into the room.
  —Go on Kullus. Go to the fire.
He stooped to the grate and stretched his fingers.
  —You do not welcome warmth,
said Kullus.
  —I?
  —There is no meeting. There is separation.
  —I have no bias.
  —You have a bias,
replied Kullus.

> You are biased towards cold. But you shut out cold and
> do not acknowledge warmth. This can on no account be
> named a fire. It is merely another aspect of light and
> shade in this room. It is not committed to its ordained
> activity. It does not move from itself, for want of an
> attention and discernment necessary to its growth. You
> live an avoidance of both elements.

  —Sit down Kullus. Take a seat.
  —I am not alone.
  —Oh?
  —I am to call, should you permit it.
I sat down on my stool.
  —Call.
At the door, Kullus called. Soon a girl was in the room,
shawled. I nodded. She nodded. She bent at the grate,
remained, rose, looked at Kullus.
  —Here, *said Kullus.*
She went to him. They climbed into my bed. I placed a coat
over the lamp, and watched the ceiling hustle to the floor.

Then the room moved to the flame in the grate. I shifted my
stool and sat by the flame in the grate.

II

Kullus took a room. The window was closed, if it was
warm, and open, if it was cold. The curtains were open, if it
was night, and closed, if it was day. Why closed? Why
open?
 —I have my night,
said Kullus.
  I have my day.
 —Do you live far from here?
asked the girl.
Kullus then opened the curtains. For the curtains were open,
if it was cold, and closed if it was warm.
I stretched my fingers to the grate.
Why open? Why closed?
 —I know cold,
said Kullus.
  I know its neighbour. Sit down. You are alone.
And so I sat down on the stool, which he placed for me.
 —You have no fire here,
I said.
Kullus moved away.
I looked at the girl. She spoke to me alone.
 —Why don't you move in here?
she asked.
  —Is it possible?
  —Can you move in here?
said the girl.
  —But how could I?
  —I will close the curtains,
said the girl.
  —But now it is night.
  —I cannot close them alone.
  —It is Kullus's night.

[94]

—Which is your room?
said the girl.

III

The curtains were closed. I crouched far from the fire.
 —What has happened to Kullus?
I asked.
  He has changed.
In her room I crouched far from the fire.
 —What has happened to Kullus?
She remained close to the grate.
 —You did not move in here,
she said.
 —No.
 —Which is your room?
she said.
 —I am no longer in my room.
The cold turned to the corner.
 —Why are you shawled?
asked the girl, and opened the curtains.
The brisk moon and the cold turned to the corner.
 —What has happened to you?
said the girl.
  You have changed.
The ceiling hustled to the floor.
 —You have not shifted the coat from the lamp,
I said.

1949

[95]

Latest Reports from the Stock Exchange

I wrote *Latest Reports from the Stock Exchange* in 1953 but lost it. It came to light recently.

In 1953 Ben Hogan was the world's top golfer and Jack Kramer one of the three top tennis players. John Foster Dulles was US secretary of state. Binkie Beaumont was the managing director of HM Tennent Ltd. Joe Lyons owned a number of Lyons Corner Houses. Gottwald was president of Czechoslovakia.

This piece was sparked by a headline in a London newspaper: 'Gottwald in coma' and my general mystification at the stock exchange reports in the stop presses of the national newspapers. HP

2.38 Amalgamated Chemicals drop one negative. All quiet on Wall Street.

2.45 Reds of the first order have infiltrated the Nursery End. I'll bet my money on the bobtail nag. Somebody bet on the bay.

3.10 The dish of the month is fatal.

LATE FLASH

Mustard in Cannon Street two pips. God works and Hitler is dead. Pigiron has jumped. Collarstuds have jumped.

3.18 All shares in the Yellow Book kaput.

3.27 National Security Loan caught on the legside. The Vatican has jumped.

LATE FLASH

Reds are reported missing. Denials are pouring in.

3.33 Gottwald in coma. Raining in Manchester. Anglo-Iranian eighty-three for eight. Bethlehem Steel has jumped.

3.41 Truce reported gathering off Gulf Stream. Shirt tails are down $3\frac{3}{8}$. Reds enforce collapse on cattlemarket.

3.48 All quiet on Wall Street.

FLASH

Minister of Finance has jumped.

3.56 Underpants in balance at Bucharest. Traffic at stand-still.

4.12 Gottwald up $2\frac{1}{2}$ accompanied by John Foster Dulles, walked the distance.

FLASH

Hitler dead and God has jumped. Betting closed on the bay. Reds scoring against the clock.

4.24 All quiet on Wall Street.

5.15 Situation still regarded in high quarters as critical. Hogan is five down at the seventh, Kramer has lost three straight to Zinc and Wall Street is volcanic. The Reds have cleaned out the sheep pens and are seven up with three to go.

FLASH

At the eighth the bobtail and the dish of the month lead a large field.

5.30 Gottwald in coma. John Foster Dulles has jumped. Exchequer Bond seventy-eight behind with two wickets in hand.

5.45 No play before lunch.

5.50 Reports that Jews have jumped denied in Rome.

5.55 Six crossdoubles with American Can for a place.

Prudential declare at overnight score. Hogan eight down at the tenth.

6.10 All quiet on Wall Street.

6.12 Floods at the eighteenth. Bobtail pipped 100–6. Gottwald in coma.

Jews have jumped. Binkie Beaumont has jumped. Bank of England and Joe Lyons collide at water jump. God has jumped back.

6.30 Moscow nine for seventy-one including the hat trick.

1953

[98]

The Black and White

I always catch the all-night bus, six days out of the week. I walk to Marble Arch and get the 294, that takes me to Fleet Street. I never speak to the men on the all-night buses. Then I go into the Black and White at Fleet Street and sometimes my friend comes. I have a cup of tea. She is taller than me but thinner. Sometimes she comes and we sit at the top table. I always keep her place but you can't always keep it. I never speak to them when they take it. Some remarks I never listen to. A man slips me the morning paper sometimes, the first one. He told me what he was once. I never go down to the place near the Embankment. I did go down there once. You can see what goes on from the window by the top table if you look. Mostly it's vans. They're always rushing. Mostly they're the same van-drivers, sometimes they're different. My brother was the same. He used to be in on it. But I can do better without the night, when it's dark, it's always light in the Black and White, sometimes it's blue, I can't see much. But I can do better without the cold when it's cold. It's always warm in the Black and White, sometimes it's draughty. I don't kip. Five o'clock they close down to give it a scrub round. I always wear my grey skirt and my red scarf, you never see me without lipstick. Sometimes my friend comes, she always brings over two teas. If there's someone taken her place she tells him. She's older than me but thinner. If it's cold I might have soup. You get a good bowl. They give you the slice of bread. They won't do that with tea but they do it with soup. So I might have soup, if it's cold. Now and again you can see the all-night buses going down. They all run down there. I've never been the other way, not the way some of them go. I've been down to Liverpool Street. That's where some of them end up. She's greyer than me. The lights get you down a bit. Once a man stood up and made a speech. A copper came in. They got him out. Then the copper came over to us. We soon told him off, my friend did. I never seen him since, either of them. They don't get many coppers. I'm a bit old for that, my friend told him. Are you, he said. Too old for you, she said. He went. I don't mind, there's not too much noise, there's always a bit of noise. Young people in cabs come in once. She didn't like the coffee. I've never had the coffee. I had coffee up at Euston, a time or two, going back. I like the vegetable soup better than the tomato. I was having a bowl then and this man was leaning from across the table, dead asleep, but sitting on his elbows, scratching his head. He was pulling the hairs out of his head into my soup, dead asleep. I pulled my bowl away. But at five o'clock they close down to give it a scrub round. They don't let you stay. My friend never stays, if she's there. You can't buy a cup of tea. I've asked but they won't let you sit, not even with your feet up. Still, you can get about four hours out of it. They only shut hour and a half. You could go down to that one near the Embankment, but I've only been down there once. I've always got my red scarf. I'm never without lipstick. I give them a look. They never pick me up. They took my friend away in the wagon once. They didn't keep her. She said they took a fancy to her. I've never gone in for that. You keep yourself clean. Still, she won't stand for any of it in the Black and White. But they don't try much. I see them look. Mostly nobody looks. I don't know many, some I've seen about. One woman in a big black hat and big black boots comes in. I never make out what she has. He slips her the morning paper. It's not long. You can go along, then come back. When it's light I go. My friend won't wait. She goes. I don't mind. One got me sick. Came in a fur coat once. They give you injections, she said, it's all Whitehall, they got it all worked out, she said, they can tap your breath, they inject you in the ears. My friend came later. She was a bit nervy. I got her quiet. They'd take her in. When it's light I walk up to the Aldwych. They're selling the papers. I've read it. One morning I went a bit over Waterloo Bridge. I saw the last 296. It must have been the last. It didn't look like an all-night bus, in daylight.

1954–5

The Examination

When we began, I allowed him intervals. He expressed no desire for these, nor any objection. And so I took it upon myself to adjudge their allotment and duration. They were not consistent, but took alteration with what I must call the progress of our talks. With a chalk I kept I marked the proposed times upon the blackboard, before the beginning of a session, for him to examine, and to offer any criticism if he felt so moved. But he made no objection, nor, during our talks, expressed any desire for a break in the proceedings. However, as I suspected they might benefit both of us, I allowed him intervals.

The intervals themselves, when they occurred, at whatever juncture, at whatever crucial point, preceded by whatever deadlock, were passed, naturally, in silence. It was not uncommon for them to be both preceded and followed by an equal silence, but this is not to say that on such occasions their purpose was offended. Frequently his disposition would be such that little could be achieved by insistence, or by persuasion. When Kullus was disposed to silence I invariably acquiesced, and prided myself on those occasions with tactical acumen. But I did not regard these silences as intervals, for they were not, and neither, I think, did Kullus so regard them. For if Kullus fell silent, he did not cease to participate in our examination. Never, at any time, had I reason to doubt his active participation, through word and through silence, between interval and interval, and I recognized what I took to be his devotion as actual and unequivocal, besides, as it seemed to me, obligatory. And so the nature of our silence within the frame of our examination, and the nature of our silence outside the frame of our examination, were entirely opposed.

Upon my announcement of an interval Kullus would

change, or act in such a manner as would suggest change. His behaviour, on these occasions, was not consistent, nor, I am convinced, was it initiated by motives of resentment or enmity, although I suspect Kullus was aware of my watchfulness. Not that I made any pretence to be otherwise. I was obliged to remark, and, if possible, to verify, any ostensible change in his manner, whether it was outside the frame of our examination or not. And it is upon this point that I could be accused of error. For gradually it appeared that these intervals proceeded according to his terms. And where both allotment and duration had rested with me, and had become my imposition, they now proceeded according to his dictates, and became his imposition.

For he journeyed from silence to silence, and I had no course but to follow. Kullus's silence, where he was entitled to silence, was compounded of numerous characteristics, the which I duly noted. But I could not always follow his courses, and where I could not follow, I was no longer his dominant.

Kullus's predilection for windows was not assumed. At every interval he retired to the window, and began from its vantage, as from a source. On approaching initially, when the break was stated, he paid no attention to the aspect beyond, either in day-time or in night-time. And only in his automatic course to the window, and his lack of interest in the aspect beyond, did he prove consistent.

Neither was Kullus's predilection for windows a deviation from former times. I had myself suffered under his preoccupation upon previous occasions, when the order of his room had been maintained by particular arrangement of window and curtain, according to day and to night, and seldom to my taste or my comfort. But now he maintained no such order and did not determine their opening or closing. For we were no longer in Kullus's room.

And the window was always open, and the curtains were always open.

Not that Kullus displayed any interest in this constant

arrangement, in the intervals, when he might note it. But as I suspect he was aware of my watchfulness, so I suspect he was aware of my arrangement. Dependent on the intensity of his silence I could suspect and conclude, but where his silence was too deep for echo, I could neither suspect nor conclude. And so gradually, where this occurred, I began to take the only course open to me, and terminated the intervals arbitrarily, cutting short the proposed duration, when I could no longer follow him, and was no longer his dominant.

But this was not until later.

When the door opened. When Kullus, unattended, entered, and the interim ended. I turned from all light in the window, to pay him due regard and welcome. Whereupon without reserve or hesitation, he moved from the door as from shelter, and stood in the light from the window. So I watched the entrance become vacant, which had been his shelter. And observed the man I had welcomed, he having crossed my border.

Equally, now, I observed the selected properties, each in its place; the blackboard, the window, the stool. And the door had closed and was absent, and of no moment. Imminent upon opening and welcoming it had possessed moment. Now only one area was to witness activity and to suffer procedure, and that only was necessary and valid. For the door was closed and so closed.

Whereupon I offered Kullus the stool, the which I placed for him. He showed, at this early juncture, no disregard for my directions; if he did not so much obey, he extended his voluntary co-operation. This was sufficient for my requirements. That I detected in him a desire for a summation of our efforts spoke well for the progress of our examination. It was my aim to avoid the appearance of subjection; a common policy, I understand, in like examinations. Yet I was naturally dominant, by virtue of my owning the room; he having entered through the door I now closed. To be confronted with the especial properties of my abode, bearing the seal and arrangement of their tenant, allowed only for recognition on the part of my visitor, and through recognition to acknowledgement, and through acknowledgement to appreciation, and through appreciation to subservience. At least, I trusted that such a development would take place, and initially believed it to have done so. It must be said, however, that his manner, from time to time, seemed to border upon indifference, yet I was not deluded by this, or offended. I viewed it as a utility he was compelled, and entitled, to fall back on, and equally as a tribute to my own incisiveness and patience. And if then I viewed it as a tactical measure, it caused me little concern. For it seemed, at this time, that the advantage was mine. Had not Kullus been obliged to attend this examination? And was not his attendance an admission of that obligation? And was not his admission an acknowledgement of my position? And my position therefore a position of dominance? I calculated this to be so, and no early event caused me to reassess this calculation. Indeed, so confident was I in the outcome of our talks, that I decided to allow him intervals.

To institute these periods, seemed to me both charitable and politic. For I hoped he might benefit from a period of no demand, so be better equipped for the periods of increased demand which would follow. And, for a time, I had no reason to doubt the wisdom of this arrangement. Also, the context of the room in which Kullus moved during the intervals was familiar and sympathetic to me, and not so to him. For Kullus had known it, and now knew it no longer, and took his place in it as a stranger, and when each break was stated, was compelled to pursue a particular convention and habit in his course, so as not to become hopelessly estranged within its boundaries. But gradually it became apparent that only in his automatic course to the window, and his lack of interest in the aspect beyond, did he prove consistent.

Prior to his arrival, I had omitted to establish one property in the room, which I knew to be familiar to him, and so liable to bring him ease. And never once did he remark the absence of a flame in the grate. I concluded he did not recognize this absence. To balance this, I emphasized the presence of the stool, indeed, placed it for him, but as he never once remarked this presence, I concluded his concern did not embrace it. Not that it was at any time simple to determine by what particular his concern might be engaged. However, in the intervals, when I was able to observe him with possibly a finer detachment, I hoped to determine this.

Until his inconsistency began to cause me alarm, and his silence to confound me.

I can only assume Kullus was aware, on these occasions, of the scrutiny of which he was the object, and was persuaded to resist it, and to act against it. He did so by deepening the intensity of his silence, and by taking courses I could by no means follow, so that I remained isolated, and outside his silence, and thus of negligible influence. And so I took the only course open to me, and terminated the intervals arbitrarily, cutting short the proposed duration, when I could no longer follow him, and was no longer his dominant.

For where the intervals had been my imposition, they had now become his imposition.

Kullus made no objection to this adjustment, though without doubt he noted my anxiety. For I suffered anxiety with good cause, out of concern for the progress of our talks, which now seemed to me to be affected. I was no longer certain whether Kullus participated in our examination, nor certain whether he still understood that as being the object of our meeting. Equally, the nature of our silences, which formerly were distinct in their opposition; that is, a silence within the frame of our examination, and a silence outside the frame of our examination; seemed to me no longer opposed, indeed were indistinguishable, and were one silence, dictated by Kullus.

And so the time came when Kullus initiated intervals at his own inclination, and pursued his courses at will, and I was able to remark some consistency in his behaviour. For now I followed him in his courses without difficulty, and there was no especial duration for interval or examination, but one duration, in which I participated. My devotion was actual and unequivocal. I extended my voluntary co-operation, and made no objection to procedure. For I desired a summation of our efforts. And when Kullus remarked the absence of a flame in the grate, I was bound to acknowledge this. And when he remarked the presence of the stool, I was equally bound. And when he removed the blackboard, I offered no criticism. And when he closed the curtains I did not object.

For we were now in Kullus's room.

1955

Tea Party

My eyes are worse.

My physician is an inch under six feet. There is a grey strip in his hair, one, no more. He has a brown stain on his left cheek. His lampshades are dark blue drums. Each has a golden rim. They are identical. There is a deep black burn in his Indian carpet. His staff is bespectacled, to a woman. Through the blinds I hear the birds of his garden. Sometimes his wife appears, in white.

He is clearly sceptical on the subject of my eyes. According to him my eyes are normal, perhaps even better than normal. He finds no evidence that my sight is growing worse.

My eyes are worse. It is not that I do not see. I do see.

My job goes well. My family and I remain close friends. My two sons are my closest friends. My wife is closer. I am close friends with all my family, including my mother and my father. Often we sit and listen to Bach. When I go to Scotland I take them with me. My wife's brother came once, and was useful on the trip.

I have my hobbies, one of which is using a hammer and nails, or a screwdriver and screws, or various saws, on wood, constructing things or making things useful, finding a use for an object which appears to have no value. But it is not so easy to do this when you see double, or when you are blinded by the object, or when you do not see at all, or when you are blinded by the object.

My wife is happy. I use my imagination in bed. We love with the light on. I watch her closely, she watches me. In the morning her eyes shine. I can see them shining through her spectacles.

All winter the skies were bright. Rain fell at night. In the morning the skies were bright. My backhand flip was my strongest weapon. Taking position to face my wife's brother, across the deal table, my bat lightly clasped, my wrist flexing, I waited to loosen my flip to his forehand, watch him (*shocked*) dart and be beaten, flounder and sulk. My forehand was not so powerful, so swift. Predictably, he attacked my forehand. There was a ringing sound in the room, a rubber sound in the walls. Predictably, he attacked my forehand. But once far to the right on my forehand, and my weight genuinely disposed, I could employ my backhand flip, un-answerable, watch him flounder, skid and be beaten. They were close games. But it is not now so easy when you see the pingpong ball double, or do not see it at all or when, hurtling towards you at speed, the ball blinds you.

I am pleased with my secretary. She knows the business well and loves it. She is trustworthy. She makes calls to Newcastle and Birmingham on my behalf and is never fobbed off. She is respected on the telephone. Her voice is persuasive. My partner and I agree that she is of inestimable value to us. My partner and my wife often discuss her when the three of us meet for coffee or drinks. Neither of them, when discussing Wendy, can speak highly enough of her.

On bright days, of which there are many, I pull the blinds in my office in order to dictate. Often I touch her swelling body. She reads back, flips the page. She makes a telephone call to Birmingham. Even were I, while she speaks (holding the receiver lightly, her other hand poised for notes) to touch her swelling body, her call would still be followed to its conclusion. It is she who bandages my eyes, while I touch her swelling body.

I do not remember being like my sons in any way when I was a boy. Their reserve is remarkable. They seem stirred by no passion. They sit silent. An odd mutter passes between them. I can't hear you, what are you saying, speak up, I say. My wife says the same. I can't hear you, what are you saying, speak up. They are of an age. They work well at school, it appears. But at pingpong both are duds. As a boy I was wide awake, of passionate interests, voluble, responsive, and my eyesight was excellent. They resemble me in no way. Their eyes are glazed and evasive behind their spectacles.

My brother-in-law was best man at our wedding. None of my friends were at that time in the country. My closest friend, who was the natural choice, was called away suddenly on business. To his great regret, he was therefore forced to opt out. He had prepared a superb speech in honour of the groom, to be delivered at the reception. My brother-in-law could not of course himself deliver it, since it referred to the long-standing friendship which existed between Atkins and myself, and my brother-in-law knew little of me. He was therefore confronted with a difficult problem. He solved it by making his sister his central point of reference. I still have the present he gave me, a carved pencil sharpener, from Bali.

The day I first interviewed Wendy she wore a tight tweed skirt. Her left thigh never ceased to caress her right, and vice versa. All this took place under her skirt. She seemed to me the perfect secretary. She listened to my counsel wide-eyed and attentive, her hands calmly clasped, trim, bulgy, plump, rosy, swelling. She was clearly the possessor of an active and inquiring intelligence. Three times she cleaned her spectacles with a silken kerchief.

After the wedding my brother-in-law asked my dear wife to remove her glasses. He peered deep into her eyes. You have married a good man, he said. He will make you happy. As he was doing nothing at the time I invited him to join me in the business. Before long he became my partner, so keen was his industry, so sharp his business acumen.

Wendy's commonsense, her clarity, her discretion, are of inestimable value to our firm.

With my eye at the keyhole I hear goosing, the squeak of them. The slit is black, only the sliding gussle on my drum, the hiss and flap of their bliss. The room sits on my head, my skull creased on the brass and loathsome handle I dare not twist, for fear of seeing black screech and scrape of my secretary writhing blind in my partner's paunch and jungle.

My wife reached down to me. Do you love me, she asked. I do love you, I spat into her eyeball. I shall prove it yet, I shall prove it yet, what proof yet, what proof remaining, what proof not yet given. All proof. (For my part, I decided on a more cunning, more allusive stratagem.) Do you love me, was my counter.

The pingpong table streaked with slime. My hands pant to gain the ball. My sons watch. They cheer me on. They are loud in their loyalty. I am moved. I fall back on strokes, on gambits, long since gone, flip, cut, chop, shtip, bluff to my uttermost. I play the ball by nose. The twins hail my efforts gustily. But my brother-in-law is no chump. He slams again, he slams again, deep to my forehand. I skid, flounder, stare sightless into the crack of his bat.

Where are my hammers, my screws, my saws?

How are you? asked my partner. Bandage on straight? Knots tight?

The door slammed. Where was I? In the office or at home? Had someone come in as my partner went out? Had he gone out? Was it silence I heard, this scuffle, creak, squeal, scrape, gurgle and muff? Tea was being poured. Heavy thighs (Wendy's? My wife's? both? apart? together?) trembled in stilettos. I sipped the liquid. It was welcome. My physician greeted me warmly. In a minute, old chap, we'll take off those bandages. Have a rock cake. I declined. The birds are at the bird bath, called his white wife. They all rushed to look. My sons sent something flying. *Someone?* Surely not. I had never heard my sons in such good form. They chattered, chuckled, discussed their work eagerly with their uncle. My parents were silent. The room seemed very small, smaller than I had remembered it. I knew where everything was, every particular. But its smell had altered. Perhaps because the room was overcrowded. My wife broke gasping out of a fit of laughter, as she was wont to do in the early days of our marriage. Why was she laughing? Had someone told her a joke? Who? Her sons? Unlikely. My sons were discussing their work with my physician and his wife. Be with you in a minute, old chap, my physician called to me. Meanwhile my partner had the two women half stripped on a convenient rostrum. Whose body swelled most? I had forgotten. I picked up a pingpong ball. It was hard. I wondered how far he had stripped the women. The top halves or the bottom halves? Or perhaps he was now raising his spectacles to view my wife's swelling buttocks, the swelling breasts of my secretary. How could I verify this? By movement, by touch. But that was out of the question. And could such a sight possibly take place under the eyes of my own children? Would they continue to chat and chuckle, as they still did, with my physician? Hardly. However, it was good to have the bandage on straight and the knots tight.

1963

The Coast

I saw him again today. He looked older.

We walked, as we always used to do, along the promenade, up to the pier, along the pier, back down the pier, and back. He was more or less more or less the same, but looked older. I asked him if I had changed. He said no, as far as he could see. I said no, probably I had not. He said he could see no sign of it, if anything I looked younger. I charged him with jesting. He said no he was not. He pointed out that he had used the phrase *if anything*. *If anything*, he said, and turned his eyes, still bright, on me, *if anything*, you look younger, *if anything*. If anything you look older, I said. There's no if anything about that, he retorted, none whatsoever.

We took the path we always took, wetter than ever along the cliff. Seems wetter than ever down here, he said, uproar in the Channel? How can you put up with such lousy weather? After all these years? Doesn't it oppress you? Not at all, I replied, most congenial, suits me. Do you still have nightmares? he asked. I smiled, into the wind. I haven't had a dream since 1956, I said. Bloody shocking racket you used to make, he said, drowning or something, God what an aggravation. He spat into the fret. One hour in this bloody wet end of the world is enough for me, don't know how you've survived, but nevertheless I'm glad to see you blossoming. Blossoming, I said, no, not quite that, surely, you're jesting.

But he had stopped talking. He was looking down at the sea, the sea he had known so well, the roar of our youth.

He bought me tea at the railway station. I then walked with him to his train. Glad to see you've found your feet, he said, glad to see you're blossoming. I clasped his hand and thanked him for making the journey.

1975

Problem

The phone rings. I ignore it. It persists. I'm not a fool. The stratagem I employ comes easily to me. I lift the extension. I say nothing. Silence too, at his end. He replaces his receiver. Remarkably harsh dialling tone.

After seeing to a few odd jobs I decide to make a telephone call. I lift the phone. Dead silence. Unprecedented. The telephone system in my area normally *sans pareil*. At the report of the slightest fault telephone technicians arrive post haste, on the dot, to correct. But in this case problem palpable. I can't phone to declare the fault, the fault is so vast, so pervasive, it so consumes, is so final, as to obstruct, without a chink of hope, aid.

Silent phone. Dead night.

The extension? Phone off hook? The extension phone off hook? I investigate. Extension secure, with a certain indolence, on hook. I am nonplussed. Not only that. I take one of my seats and sit nonplussed.

Nonplussed. No tone. Dead night.

It rings.

*

I leave the library, go into a phone box and dial my flat. Number engaged.

*

Someone is trying to do me in.

1976

Lola

After he had gone, I pondered on all he was evidently keeping from me. The information I had received from him was insufficient for me to do more than subject it to the broadest and most superficial analysis. The information I had received from him, meagre, banal, threadbare, misleading or, where precise, outlandish, did me in fact precious little damn bloody good. He was on a train, he said, leaving the Gare de Lyon; dozens of lines crossed; an exquisite arrangement of train upon train, crossing, deflecting, genuflecting, quite the most courteous choreography ever encountered by the witness, who then remarked the lurching silver train, undoubtedly bound for the Côte d'Azur, cheek to cheek with his own, and in the azure window (sunset, or dawn, scattered upon the pane) the darkeyed, darkhaired girl he had known, and loved, when a boy, long gone, long last seen, dancing so lightly in his young arms, amid flowering plants. It was love at second sight, confirmed, tattooed between them on golden windows (a moment when dawn and sunset glided together in summer must) her eyes her hair so lost in shocking seconds graze of light on departing Paris gone. But that cannot be all. He has left me to ponder on all he has kept from me.

Saw Smith again. What rubbish. Why do I go there? Up his old stairs, the long wait for the door to open, the door opens, always the hesitation, oh hello, door kept ajar, oh hello, oh it's you, what a surprise, thought it was Lola, come in, we go in, we stand, thought it might be Lola, you can never tell when she might take it into her head to embark on another sally, sit down, sit, sit, tell me, willy nilly, all that is momentous in your life.

I tell him this: I am very happy in my house in the country and my life as a countryman. I enjoy long walks by the side of the river. It is autumn. The life of the countryside delights me, the life of birds, of ducks. I watch boys fishing. They often fish with their fathers, at their side tins of sandwiches cut by their mothers. There is no end to boats. They disappear upstream in a long wake. So easeful their progress, wide their wake. There is no scar on my landscape. I gain no pleasure whatsoever from my journeys to London, apart from seeing my oldest friend, you. I remain so closely interested in you. I think of you late at night, in my study, over my brandy. I imagine you sitting amid your candles and lilies, keeping your solitary wake. No candle I know holds a candle to your candles.

I think that I might write of you, make of you the central figure of a modest novella; modest since I doubt I could ever fully capture the heart of your character, never precisely clench you within my noose, so to speak. I see you only in the shuddering of candles, an old man, one who had never known boyhood, or other distinctions of light. My respect for you rests in the fact that you do not waver, that your patience does not waver, since, your life rapidly failing, you sit in your room paying unwavering attention to the Lola of your wavering candles. My contempt for you follows from this. My contempt for you rests in the fact that you wait only for tightskirted Lola to enter, wait only for the exquisite collision of you with her bouncing flamboyant bellbottomed bottom, the collision that will be the end of you.

He responds: Tell me more about the train incident.

What train incident?

The incident which contained a darkeyed darkhaired girl, in a train leaving Paris, in a window, passing. A dawning sunset. You both had loved, years before. She looked at you, through grazing light. You saw. She had not forgotten you. When you had last seen her she cried, you touched her wrist, she buried her head, you withdrew your hand. All this took place miles away, long before you embarked on your trip to this room.

Can I for much longer tolerate the insults to which he subjects me?

1977

Short Story

There was another daughter who died. I'm thinking of
finding out a little more about that. We had no connection.
I came from another family, a totally different family. She
didn't dandle me on her knee or anything like that. She wasn't
my mother. She died and went to heaven. I don't know what
she looked like. It was all rumour and addenda, probably lies
anyway. Hardly a matter of life or death. Apart from the fact
that she did die. But that applies to everybody.

That afternoon I sipped a glass of beer in a pub. Then I
walked along the beach, among the rocks, through the tide,
amid the jetsam and the flotsam, all that. The echo chamber
of the dead and drowned, the ones who spoke perfect English
and now sport rapidly blackening lipstick. The ones with
thighs up to their waist and breasts like turbot – some people
would say tits like turbot but not me.

I walk along the beach and think of the one who died. She was
one of the daughters who died. She was another daughter,
faceless, an obscure member of a substantial and highly
respected family. She was absolutely no relation. I never
even kissed her on her soft cheek, not even when she was
young, not even when she was a young girl, breasts like
turbot, that kind of thing.

1995

Girls

I read this short story in a magazine where a girl student goes into her professor's office and sits at his desk and passes him a note which he opens and which reads: 'Girls like to be spanked.' But I've lost it. I've lost the magazine. I can't find it. And I can't remember what happened next. I don't even know whether the story was fiction or fact. It may have been an autobiographical fragment. But from whose point of view was the story told? The professor's or the girl's? I don't know. I can't remember. The blinding ignorance I am now experiencing is the clearest and cleanest road to madness. What I want to know is quite simple. Was she spanked? If, that is, she was including herself in her all-embracing proposition. If she was including herself in her all-embracing proposition, did she, personally, benefit from it? Was she, not to put too fine a point on it, one of those girls? Was she, or is she, one of those girls who, according to her account, like to be spanked? If that was the case, did it happen? Did it happen in the professor's office, on the professor's desk? Or not? And what about the professor? What did he make of it all? What kind of professor was he, anyway? What was his discipline? Did he subject the assertion (girls like to be spanked) to serious critical scrutiny? Did he find it a dubious generalization or, at any rate, did he set out to verify it? Did he, in other words, put it to the test? Did he, for example, in other words, say: 'OK. Lie on my desk, bottom up, face averted, and let us both determine whether there is substance to this assertion or not?' Or did he simply warn the student, in the interests of science, to tread warily for ever more, in the perilous field of assertion?

The trouble is, I can't find the magazine. I've lost it. And I've no idea how the story – or the autobiographical fragment – developed. Did they fall in love? Did they marry? Did they give birth to lots of little animals?

A man or woman or both must have written this piece about a girl who walks into her professor's office and sits at his desk and passes him a note which he opens and which reads: 'Girls like to be spanked.' But I don't know his or her name; I don't know the author's identity. And I simply don't know whether the girl was in fact spanked, there and then, without further ado, in the professor's office, on his desk, or at any other time, on someone else's desk, here, there, everywhere, all the time, on the hour, religiously, tenderly, fervently, ceaselessly, for ever and for ever and for ever. But it's also possible that she wasn't talking about herself. She might not necessarily have meant that *she* liked to be spanked. She may just have been talking about other girls, girls she didn't even know, millions of girls she hadn't even met, would never meet, millions of girls she hadn't in fact ever actually heard of, millions and billions of girls on the other side of the world who, in her view, liked, simply, without beating about the bush, to be spanked. Or on the other hand she may have been talking about other girls, girls born at Cockfosters or studying American Literature at the University of East Anglia, who had actually told her personally, in breathtaking spasms of spectacular candour, that they, when all was said but nothing yet done, liked, when the chips were down, nothing better than to be spanked. In other words, her assertion (girls like to be spanked) might have been the climax of a long, deep, thoroughly researched course of study she had undertaken honourably and had honourably concluded.

I love her. I love her so much. I think she's a wonderful woman. I saw her once. She turned and smiled. She looked at me and smiled. Then she wiggled to a cab in the cab rank. She gave instructions to the cab driver, opened the door, got in, closed the door, glanced at me for the last time through the window and the cab drove off and I never saw her again.

1995

[III]

School Life

I'm one of the barrow boys
he said. Kedge,
his big hands inkstained,
and laughed. They
stood, gumbooted. The
Shakespearean tragedians.
Scuffling, the dust
rose and the floorboards
creaked. Someone will
come in in a minute.
One smelt of flannel
trousers and shredded wheat.
In the corridor, they sweep,
their cloaks sweeping.

Dumb fingers over stained
pages. The fountain pens
of the damned.
The lewd jokes of Godfrey
Up with the radiator heat
and someone's bad breath.
How plead the wicked?
To prove: x. Given?
You will say it is merely
a periphrastic conjugation.
It is not.

A new one. Who is he?
Cold glasses, aloof stare.
What is he like?
Dangerous. The word
went round the clubs.

It is really like a castle.
Descending the stairs dark.

They stand in the doorway.
Oh, for God's sake.
Get out. Get out.
The corridor coldness. In the library
we meet.

There is *Trois Contes* on
the bottom shelf.
Harris, smiling, silky. I
met him in the Ritz bar,
my dear boy. Keys scrape
dust off the windowsill.
I want my dinner you
poetasters.
From the Greek?

1948

At the Palace of the Emperor at Dawn

The eighteenth-century doctor
Covers with leeches the broken nostrils,
Both madman and alchemist conjure
The screaming sky.
Indigo flatters the eye.
Now coy marionettes
Like snails unbend.
Another Parthenon crumbles in sand.
But still the snail of love
Suns the decks.
At Quadragesima in March
Bubbles shutter the frogs
In transparent sacks.
At Martinmas November stoat
In nightmare claws a lover's thighs.
Eyes gnaw the hedge's coat.

Stone quiet – time a mirage,
Buried the world
In the molten Japanese village.
The wooden gong in the Temple strikes
Where the rice falls apart,
Shattering the beads, the mangoes,
All bloom at the start.
And now we hear the distress of silence.

1949

Once, in a Ventriloquist Evening

Once, in a ventriloquist evening,
When winter scoffed the dummy head,
Said God your messenger is dead,
The lines are cut, and all the roads
Are snaked, I,
Bullseyed under a mosslamp,
Verbed a fable to this hymning sound:

O my muckers, in your cadaverous twist,
Such an ache of antics to the tinsel tricks,
That a tit of limpet on the dissecting ape
Shall wrap you round in a funereal glint,
Bubonic among tortoise.

What was fancy is ghoul and robin
Wrecked. The world's heel rides close
To the sun. Fever and white gowns.

1949

New Year in the Midlands

Now here again she blows, landlady of lumping
Fellows between the boards,
Singing 'O Celestial Light', while
Like a T-square on the
Flood swings her wooden leg.
This is the shine, the powder and blood, and here am I,
Straddled, exile always in one Whitbread Ale town,
Or such.
Where we went to the yellow pub, cramped in an alley bin,
A shoot from the market,
And found the thin Luke of a queer, whose pale
Deliberate eyes, raincoat, Victorian,
Sap the answer in the palm.
All the crush, camp, burble and beer
Of this New Year's Night; the psalm derided;
The black little crab women with the long
Eyes, lisp and claw in a can of chockfull stuff.
I am rucked in the heat of treading; the well-rolled
Sailor boys soon rocked to sleep, whose ferret fig
So calms the coin of a day's fever.
Now in this quaver of a roisty bar, the wansome lady
I blust and stir,
Who pouts the bristle of a sprouting fag—
Sprinkled and diced in these Midland lights
Are Freda the whimping glassy bawd, and your spluttered
    guide,
Blessed with ambrosial bitter weed. – Watch
How luminous hands
Unpin the town's genitals—
Young men and old
With the beetle glance,

The crawing brass whores, the clamping
Red-shirted boy, ragefull, thudding his cage.

1950

The Midget

I saw the midget in the ringing airs,
That night upon the crest.
The bowed trees, the silent beast,
Under the wind.

And saw the voyagers stand stiff,
Deathsure, stiff and coffined
In that still place,
Hands clasped, tall hats on.

1950

Christmas

Choose the baby's cocktail,
To drink in an eartrumpet.
Deprivation angers; at least
Rejoice in his captivity.

Give Maurice lemons.
He's broken the pottery,
Arses round the attic,
Gorging biscuits and olives.

This is a happy family.
Come, sing of the harbour,
Nights guzzling bouillabaisse.
We'll syringe to the next flat,
Make another party.

1950

Chandeliers and Shadows

'I'le goe hunt the badger by owle-light: 'tis a deed of
darknesse.' *The Duchess of Malfi*

The eyes of a queen germinate
In this brothel, in this room,
The kings are fled, the potentates
Shuffle kingdoms with the sweet fingers.
Mountains, kingdoms, valets erudite,
Muffling flaunts of deliberate ecstasy
Slips, shoves, the deluded whore,
The hectoring mice, the crabs of lemon,
Scrawled thick tails across the stateroom.
Masks gape in the floodlit emperies,
Where wax violins, donkey splendour falls,
The brocaded gown of servants and moths,
The horsefly, the palsied stomacher,
Worlds dying, suns in delirium,
Catch the sleek counsellor,
Hold the crystal elixir of muffs.

Enwrapped in this crust, this crumpled mosaic,
Camphor and rosefall stifle the years,
Yet I, lunatic from lunatic spheres,
Shall run crazy with lepers,
And bring God down the chimney,
A tardy locust,
To plunder and verminate man's pastures, entirely.
Sudden I stay blinded with Orion's menace,
The sky cuts the ice-shell
With the strip and fall of a darting star,
The split, the splintered palace.
Let them all burn together

In a trite December,
A necromantic cauldron of crosses,
And on Twelfth Night the long betrayed monster
Shall gobble their gilded gondolas.

1950

Hampstead Heath

I, lying on grass, lie
in the thunderclapping moment,
eradicate voice
in the green limit.

Stone in the fruitwomb,
world under grass,
alone under alone.

Suggested lines my body
consume, in the day's graph.
Note the brown ant
in his blade jungle.

I am my pupil's blank, rule
out of magnitude the ant,
decrease the seed's activity
this blunt minute.

Below the transparent fly
insect equation quite strides
the slim glass of word,
instructs the void.

Exterior tricks: the click
of bush; the oblong trade
of noise; the posture of these
high boughs.

1951

I Shall Tear off my Terrible Cap

I in my straight jacket swung in the sun,
In a hostile pause in a no man's time.
The spring his green anchor had flung.
Around me only the walking brains,
And the plack of their onelegged dreams
As I hung.

I tell them this—
Only the deaf can hear and the blind understand
The miles I gabble.
Through these my dances of dunce and devil,
It's only the dumb can speak through the rubble.
Time shall drop his spit in my cup,
With this vicious cut he shall close my trap
And gob me up in a drunkard's lap.
All spirits shall haunt me and all devils drink me;
O despite their dark drugs and the digs that they rib me,
I'll tear off my terrible cap.

1951

A Glass at Midnight

Time of the mongrel at my foot
Scraping for a coin that's born
In the carpet in a grave of hair.

Miles of the poles in the room's corners.
The eskimostars in an octagon. Worlds
Within this box.

I hold the cipher of the voided world,
Four fingers holding the sea in a glass,
Incumbent an arm on the ashtray table.

Time in the tughoot night stops
A religion that grows on the window.
I let the glass drop. A bridge falls.
Flatten the midnight on the fingered tightrope.
All the dumb days draw on.

1951

Book of Mirrors

My book is crammed with the dead
Youths of years.

Fabulous in image I walked the Mayworlds,
Equal in favour the concubant winds,
Set by my triangle the sectant sounds,
Till crowed lips I kissed,
Supped with a blood of snapping birds,
In a doom and ring of belladonna to sleep.

Spruced, I welcomed their bone-eating smiles,
Till I grew bound and easy with ills,
Strewing for decorance a hundred grails.
And anger-rich with gallows and banks,
The world raped on her back,
From the shanks of my widowing kids
I played Adam's uncle's joke.

In the house of my heart spawned
The invited doves.
May springroot slum their hurt limbs,
That they chirp the early ladies
And prop the mad brideworld up.
May they breathe sweet; the shapes
That ounced my glad weight
With ripe and century fingers,
That locked the skeleton years
With a gained grief.

1951

The Islands of Aran Seen from the Moher Cliffs

The three whales of Aran
Humped in the sun's teeth,
Make tough bargain with the cuff
And statement of the sea.

I stand on Moher, the cliffs
Like coalvaults, see Aran
In mourning thumped to losses
By its season's neighbour.

Aran like three black whales
Humped on the water,
With a whale's barricade
Stares out the waves.

Aran with its bleak gates locked,
Its back to the traders,
Aran the widower,
Aran with no legs

Distended in distance
From the stone of Connemara's head,
Aran without gain, pebbled
In the fussing Atlantic.

1951

Others of You

By night in Drumconnan,
Spyglass bending,
Bend to the funnel of distance,
Below climate of angel and dormouse,
Centuried a memory illumine,
With silence the orator.

The always-beginning calling
In the twolegged night,
Of any the home I am,
Of many the home I make,
From this heartbeating centre
Navigate distance, to return
To others of you, conjured
Between dream and occasion.

To others of you I tender,
Make arriving tides loud down
In uncommon current, to birth
And to burial, alive in occurrence.
My inhabiting welcomed move
To a scripture, hearing the weathers
Make hourvoice and silence.
By night in Drumconnan.

1951

Episode

I

Why do you follow?

I tread their shadow,
Stranger and woman,
Arranging the season
In her curious dream.
And best announced
From my alphabet home,
Consume their echo,
Cancel the sun.

Why do you leave me?

Of three there are figures
Whose third is unechoed
Where two are alone.
And I, her follower,
Fall back to forest,
Cancel the sun.

That she carries a bowl
And selects the red stones,
That her third is unechoed,
And closebred, a stranger,
That the thunder has broken
About the round tower, I allow.
Allowing, not following,
By the animal fire.

Why do you stay with me?

The crooks of my fingers
Distribute the ash.
She, widowed; her third,
Her third is her lover.
She, widowed, unsighted,
Her third is her stranger.

II

Come. Our two walking,
And shadows beginning,
Sauntering altered, and
The autumn bereaving.
That her third was unechoed
I could hardly allow.
By his bearing I knew him,
And our silence making,
We turned through the pillars
Of dust that enticed.

So we crouched to begin.
I counted the thunder
That leaned at my temples
And crouched to begin.
On his nail was her eyelash,
That lined the calm.

HE:

That you did barter
And consort with her.
That you did ash
The fire at her departure.
That you did enter
Where I was unechoed.
That you did venture
Where I was a stranger.
That you did cajole

When the pendulum hung.
That you interposed
In her curious dream.
That you did instruct
From your alphabet home.
That you did confusion
Her eyelid to stone.
That you so did render
The echo unheard
That you might divide
When the echo was gone.
That you did condition
Her widowhood on.
That you were the stranger
That strangered the calm.
That you did engender
The thunder to storm.
That yours was the practice.
You cancelled the sun.
I tell that you sundered
From forest, consumed
Where I watched.
Where though I stayed,
Where though I left,
I cannot decipher;
Which scarecrow she lured,
Or which pleasure took.

I:

The plunder left to us
Is a similar eyelash.

III

Why did you leave me?

Gaining through the pillars
And the thunder at my temples
And her eyes that had altered
And the silence she was made of
And the dumb word ending.

Why did you follow?

Her third is unechoed.

And I am her stranger.

1951

The Irish Shape

Not for this am I for nothing here,
But for that only I remain from her.
But for that only I should close the day,
Let the sky trade with the other skull,
But for that only and the Irish shape.
Not for this nothing do I frown this hand,
Not for this sunlight and the cage I am,
Only for this mirror and this all spring's time,
Only for the passing of the sea below,
Only for the silence, for her eyebrow.

1951

The Drama in April

So March has become a museum,
And the April curtains move.
I travel the vacant gallery
To the last seat.
In the spring décor
The actors pitch tents,
In a beak of light
Begin their play.

Their cries in the powdered dark
Assemble in mourning over
Ambassadors from the wings.
And objects and props in the rain
Are the ash of the house
And the grave unnumbered stones
In the green.

I move to the interval,
Done with this repertory.

1952

Jig

Seeing my portholed women
Fall on the murdered deck,
I rage in my iron cabin.

Faster my starboard women,
Spun by the metal breeze,
Dance to a cut-throat temper.

Seeing my men in armour
Brand the galley bark,
I skip to drydock.

Women and men together,
All in a seaquick temper,
Tick the cabin clock.

1952

The Anaesthetist's Pin

The anaesthetist's pin
Binds up the bawl of pain.
The amputator's saw
Breaks the condition down.

In the division of blood
That stems the fractured bow,
The wrist-attacking hound
Snipes out the stair below.

At that incision sound
The lout is at the throat
And the dislocated word
Becomes articulate.

1952

Camera Snaps

The politician tricks the mouse,
Whose bites are rancid
In that aloed wound.
The sun's in the cabinet.

The sun's in the cabinet.
That drudge undoes the skeleton,
And chops the scientific dug.
Light across the picture.

Dark across the picture.
The basement midget, rabid
As the stoat, periscopes
The tickshop of the moon.

The churchman at his game
Unrolls his fishing-line,
Jabs an even pool.
Dark across the cabinet.

1952

You in the Night

You in the night should hear
The thunder and the walking air.
You on that shore shall bear
Where mastering weathers are.

All that honoured hope
Shall fail upon the slate,
And break the winter down
That clamours at your feet.

Though the enamouring altars burn,
And the deliberate sun
Make the eagle bark,
You'll tread the tightrope.

c. 1952

The Second Visit

My childhood vampire wallows in those days,
Where panting sea threatened and surf was flint,
And consummate doves flanked the eyes.

Now an actor in this nocturnal sink,
The strip of lip is toothed away,
And flats and curtains canter down.

So grows in stream of planetary tides
The sun abundant in hanging sands.

And aquiline weapons barb and fanged
Conceive amid their holy jaws
An echoed Siberia in the mind,
Where the comet fist had crushed,
And sent back trees to a gulped barrenness.

Denebola and Alphard like countertenors
Sing, and their malicious minstrels of song
Silence the tongue's gush,
And the quick opus of thighs.

My childhood vampire unpacks a new stay,
But I defy and send him off to war,
On the credit of Leo and his gods,
Against the fallingdown parents
Devoured by children, and the toy Czars.

c. 1952

A Walk by Waiting

A walk by listening.
A walk by waiting.

Wait under the listening
Winter, walk by the glass.

Rest by the glass of waiting.
Walk by the season of voices.

Number the winter of flowers.
Walk by the season of voices.

Wait by the voiceless glass.

1953

Poem

I walked one morning with my only wife,
Out of sandhills to the summer fair,
To buy a window and a white shawl,
Over the boulders and the sunlit hill.
But a stranger told us the fair had passed,
And I turned back with my only wife.

And I turned back and I led her home.
She followed me closely out of the summer,
Over the boulders and the moonlit hill,
Into sandhills in the early evening,
And went to our home without a window,
And the long year moved from the east.

My only wife sat by a candle.
The winter keened at the door.
A widow brought us a long black shawl.
I placed it on my true wife's shoulders.
The widow went from us into sandhills,
Away from our home without a window.

The year turned to an early sunrise.
I walked one morning with my only wife,
Out of sandhills to the summer fair,
To sell a candle and a black shawl.
We parted ways on the sunlit hill,
She silent, I to the farther west.

1953

The Task

The last time Kullus, seen,
Within a distant call,
Arrived at the house of bells,
The leaf obeyed the bud,
I closed the open night
And tailormade the room.

The last time Kullus, known,
Obeyed a distant call,
Within the house of night,
The leaf alarmed the bud,
I closed the open bell
And tailormade the room.

The last time Kullus saw
The sun upon the bough,
And in a distant call,
The bud about to break,
I set about my task
And tailormade the room.

The last time Kullus saw
The flower begin to fail,
He made a distant call,
The bud became a bell,
I disobeyed that cry
And pacified the room.

1954

The Error of Alarm

A pulse in the dark
I could not arrest.
The error of alarm
I could not dismiss.
A witness to that bargain
I could not summon.

If his substance tautens
I am the loss of his blood.
If my thighs approve him
I am the sum of his dread.

If my eyes cajole him
That is the bargain made.
If my mouth allays him
I am his proper bride.

If my hands forestall him
He is deaf to my care.
If I own to enjoy him
The bargain's bare.

The fault of alarm
He does not share.
I die the dear ritual
And he is my bier.

1956

Daylight

I have thrown a handful of petals on your breasts.
Scarred by this daylight you lie petalstruck.
So your skin imitates the flush, your head
Turning all ways, bearing a havoc of flowers over you.

Now I bring you from dark into daytime,
Laying petal on petal.

1956

Afternoon

Summer twisted from their grasp
After the first fever.
Daily from the stews
They brought the men
And placed a wooden peg
Into the wound they had made,
And left the surgery of skin
To barbers and students.

Some burrowed for their loss
In the ironmonger's bin,
Impatient to reclaim,
Before the journey start,
Their articles of faith.

Some nosed about in the dirt,
Deaf to the smell of heat
And the men at the rubber pit,
Who scattered the parts of a goat
For their excitement and doubt.

One blind man they gave
A demented dog to sniff,
A bitch that had eaten the loot.
The dog, bare to his thought,
Became his mastiff at night,
His guardian the thief of his blood.

1957

A View of the Party

I

The thought that Goldberg was
A man she might have known
Never crossed Meg's words
That morning in the room.

The thought that Goldberg was
A man another knew
Never crossed her eyes
When, glad, she welcomed him.

The thought that Goldberg was
A man to dread and know
Jarred Stanley in the blood
When, still, he heard his name.

While Petey knew, not then,
But later, when the light
Full up upon their scene,
He looked into the room.

And by morning Petey saw
The light begin to dim
(That daylight full of sun)
Though nothing could be done.

II

Nat Goldberg, who arrived
With a smile on every face,
Accompanied by McCann,
Set a change upon the place.

The thought that Goldberg was
Sat in the centre of the room,
A man of weight and time,
To supervise the game.

The thought that was McCann
Walked in upon this feast,
A man of skin and bone,
With a green stain on his chest.

Allied in their theme,
They imposed upon the room
A dislocation and doom,
Though Meg saw nothing done.

The party they began,
To hail the birthday in,
Was generous and affable,
Though Stanley sat alone.

The toasts were said and sung,
All spoke of other years,
Lulu, on Goldberg's breast,
Looked up into his eyes.

And Stanley sat – alone,
A man he might have known,
Triumphant on his hearth,
Which never was his own.

For Stanley had no home.
Only where Goldberg was,
And his bloodhound McCann,
Did Stanley remember his name?

They played at blind man's buff,
Blindfold the game was run,
McCann tracked Stanley down,
The darkness down and gone

Found the game lost and won,
Meg, all memory gone,
Lulu's lovenight spent,
Petey impotent;

A man they never knew
In the centre of the room,
And Stanley's final eyes
Broken by McCann.

1958

The Table

I dine the longest
All this time

My feet I hear
Fall on the fat

On cheese and eggs
On weekend bones

The sound of light
Has left my nose.

Tattooed with all
I could not see

I whisper in
My deafest ear

My name erased
Was sometime here

Or total bluff
Preserved its care.

To this enchained
With this in love

I move on fours
Without a word

And stuffed with tributes
Hog the scraps

Breathless,
Under this enormous table.

1963

Poem

Always where you are
In what I do
Turning you hold your arms

My touch lies where you turn
Your look is in my eyes

Turning to clasp your arms
You hold my touch in you

Touching to clasp in you
The one shape of our look
I hold your face to me

Always where you are
My touch to love you looks into your eyes.

1964

All of That

All of that I made
And, making, lied.
And all of that I hid
Pretended dead.

But all of that I hid
Was always said,
But, hidden, spied
On others' good.

And all of that I led
By nose to bed
And, bedding, said
Of what I did

To all of that that cried
Behind my head
And, crying, died
And is not dead.

1970

Poem

they kissed I turned they stared
with bright eyes turning to me blind
I saw that here where we were joined
the light that fell upon us burned
so bright the darkness that we shared
while they with blind eyes turning to me turned
and I their blind kiss formed

1971

Later

Later. I look out at the moon.
I lived here once.
I remember the song.

Later. No sound here.
Moon on linoleum.
A child frowning.

Later. A voice singing.
I open the back door.
I lived here once.

Later. I open the back door
Light gone. Dead trees.
Dead linoleum. Later.

Later. Blackness moving very fast.
Blackness fatly.
I live here now.

1974

Poem

and all the others
wary now
attentive to flowers

and all the others
unsmiling
recalling others

smiling in gardens
attentive to flowers
wary now

who recall others
wary now
tendering flowers

who recall faces of others
recalling others
unwary in gardens

who tender their gardens
recalling others
wary with flowers

1974

Paris

The curtain white in folds,
She walks two steps and turns,
The curtain still, the light
Staggers in her eyes.

The lamps are golden.
Afternoon leans, silently.
She dances in my life.
The white day burns.

1975

I know the place

I know the place.
It is true.
Everything we do
Corrects the space
Between death and me
And you.

1975

Message

Jill. Fred phoned. He can't make tonight.
He said he'd call again, as soon as poss.
I said (on your behalf) OK, no sweat.
He said to tell you he was fine,
Only the crap, he said, you know, it sticks,
The crap you have to fight.
You're sometimes nothing but a walking shithouse.

I was well acquainted with the pong myself,
I told him, and I counselled calm.
Don't let the fuckers get you down,
Take the lid off the kettle a couple of minutes,
Go on the town, burn someone to death,
Find another tart, give her some hammer,
Live while you're young, until it palls,
Kick the first blind man you meet in the balls.

Anyway he'll call again.

I'll be back in time for tea.

Your loving mother.

1977

The Doing So

It is the test they set that will not go,
The failing of the doing so,
Ungainly legacy that they bestow.

I know the tricks and yet I cannot show
Why you and I in all our afterglow
Just fail the test of doing so.
It is the legacy that they bestow,
And they remorselessly will have it so.

It is the test of those who cannot row
Upon a burning sea where charred winds blow
The ghastly empires of the dead and tow
Them to their ghastly deaths to show
Them dead and ghastly, smiling, slow.
It is the test they set that will not go.

And all our dead and all their dead friends know
We have no gift for lying low,
No gift at all for doing so.
The test they set you will not go.
It is the legacy that they bestow,
The failing of the doing so.

1977

Denmark Hill

Well, at least you're there,
And when I come into the room,
You'll stand, your hands linked,
And smile,
Or, if asleep,
Wake.

1977

Joseph Brearley 1909–1977

(Teacher of English)

Dear Joe, I'd like to walk with you
From Clapton Pond to Stamford Hill
And on,
Through Manor House to Finsbury Park,
And back,
On the dead 653 trolleybus,
To Clapton Pond,
And walk across the shadows on to Hackney Downs,
And stop by the old bandstand,
You tall in moonlight,
And the quickness in which it all happened,
And the quick shadow in which it persists.

You're gone. I'm at your side,
Walking with you from Clapton Pond to Finsbury Park,
And on, and on.

1977

The Ventriloquists

I send my voice into your mouth
You return the compliment

I am the Count of Cannizzaro
You are Her Royal Highness the Princess Augusta

I am the thaumaturgic chain
You hold the opera glass and cards

You become extemporaneous song
I am your tutor

You are my invisible seed
I am Timour the Tartar

You are my curious trick
I your enchanted caddy

I am your confounding doll
You my confounded dummy.

1981

Poem

The lights glow.
What will happen next?

Night has fallen.
The rain stops.
What will happen next?

Night will deepen.
He does not know
What I will say to him.

When he has gone
I'll have a word in his ear
And say what I was about to say
At the meeting about to happen
Which has now taken place.

But he said nothing
At the meeting about to take place.
It is only now that he turns and smiles
And whispers:
'I do not know
What will happen next.'

1981

Ghost

I felt soft fingers at my throat
It seemed someone was strangling me

The lips were hard as they were sweet
It seemed someone was kissing me

My vital bones about to crack
I gaped into another's eyes

I saw it was a face I knew
A face as sweet as it was grim

It did not smile it did not weep
Its eyes were wide and white its skin

I did not smile I did not weep
I raised my hand and touched its cheek

1983

Before They Fall

Before they fall
The obese stars
Dumb stones dumb lumps of light

Before they gasp before they

Before they gasp
And spit out their last blood

Before they drop before they

Before they drop
In spikes of frozen fire

Before they choke before they

Before they choke
In a last heartburn of stunk light

Let me say this

1983

Poem

I saw Len Hutton in his prime

Another time

another time

1986

It Is Here
(for A)

What sound was that?

I turn away, into the shaking room.

What was that sound that came in on the dark?
What is this maze of light it leaves us in?
What is this stance we take,
To turn away and then turn back?
What did we hear?

It was the breath we took when we first met.

Listen. It is here.

1990

American Football

A Reflection upon the Gulf War

Hallelujah!
It works.
We blew the shit out of them.

We blew the shit right back up their own ass
And out their fucking ears.

It works.
We blew the shit out of them.
They suffocated in their own shit!

Hallelujah.
Praise the Lord for all good things.

We blew them into fucking shit.
They are eating it.

Praise the Lord for all good things.

We blew their balls into shards of dust,
Into shards of fucking dust.

We did it.

Now I want you to come over here and kiss me on the mouth.

1991

God

God looked into his secret heart
To find a word
To bless the living throng below.

But look and look as he might do
And begging ghosts to live again
But hearing no song in that room
He found with harshly burning pain
He had no blessing to bestow.

1993

Poem

Don't look.
The world's about to break.

Don't look.
The world's about to chuck out all its light
And stuff us in the chokepit of its dark,
That black and fat and suffocated place
Where we will kill or die or dance or weep
Or scream or whine or squeak like mice
To renegotiate our starting price.

1995

Cricket at Night

They are still playing cricket at night
They are playing the game in the dark
They're on guard for a backlash of light

They are losing the ball at long leg
They are trying to learn how the dark
Helps the yorker knock back the off-peg

They are trying to find a new trick
Where the ball moves to darkness from light
They're determined to paint the scene black
But a blackness compounded by white
They are dying to pass a new law
Where blindness is deemed to be sight

They are still playing cricket at night

1995

The Other Guy

It's the other guy who's dying
He's turning in his grave
He's dead but goes on living
His price is on his sleeve

He swears that he is holy
As he rats upon his life
But admits that he is banking
On the battle-scarred procedures
Of his last bad breath

To glue him to a country
Where the girls and boys contend
That the dead come back from dying
But that there is an end

To the ducking and the weaving
The frenzy and the scrum
The itching and the scratching
The sucking-back of scum

It's the other guy who's dying
He's dying out of love
A love that holds him breathless
And burns him in his grave

1995

Order

Are you ready to order?

No there is nothing to order
No I'm unable to order
No I'm a long way from order

And while there is everything,
And nothing, to order,
Order remains a tall order

And disorder feeds on the belly of order
And order requires the blood of disorder
And 'freedom' and ordure and other disordures
Need the odour of order to sweeten their murders

Disorder a beggar in a darkened room
Order a banker in a castiron womb
Disorder an infant in a frozen home
Order a soldier in a poisoned tomb

1996

The Old Days

Well, there was no problem.
All the democracies
(all the democracies)

were behind us.

So we had to kill some people.
So what?
Lefties get killed.

This is what we used to say
back in the old days:

Your daughter is a lefty

I'll ram this stinking battering-ram
all the way up and up and up and up
right the way through all the way up
all the way through her lousy lefty body.

So that stopped the lefties.

They may have been the old days
but I'll tell you they were the good old days.

Anyway all the democracies
(all the democracies)
were behind us.

They said: just don't
(just don't)
tell anyone we're behind you.

That's all.
Just don't tell anyone
(just don't)
just don't tell anyone
we're behind you.

Just kill them.

Well, my wife wanted peace.
And so did my little children.
So we killed all the lefties
to bring peace for our little children.

Anyway there was no problem.
Anyway they're all dead anyway.

1996

Death

(Births and Deaths Registration Act 1953)

Where was the dead body found?
Who found the dead body?
Was the dead body dead when found?
How was the dead body found?

Who was the dead body?

Who was the father or daughter or brother
Or uncle or sister or mother or son
Of the dead and abandoned body?

Was the body dead when abandoned?
Was the body abandoned?
By whom had it been abandoned?

Was the dead body naked or dressed for a journey?

What made you declare the dead body dead?
Did you declare the dead body dead?
How well did you know the dead body?
How did you know the dead body was dead?

Did you wash the dead body
Did you close both its eyes
Did you bury the body
Did you leave it abandoned
Did you kiss the dead body

1997

The Disappeared

Lovers of light, the skulls,
The burnt skin, the white
Flash of the night,
The heat in the death of men.

The hamstring and the heart
Torn apart in a musical room,
Where children of the light
Know that their kingdom has come.

1998

Requiem for 1945

It was like they always said,
The blind, the dumb, the left for dead,
The long believers of the night,
The grandads who looked out to light
But found the portholes of their room
Smashed by a sea that snarled at them
And drowned and snatched away their air
To punish them for their desire.

1999

They All Rang

When I moved
I sent a card to those who'd want to know
Where I live now.

David Mercer, Pat McGee,
Joseph Losey, Peggy Ashcroft,
Donald Pleasence, Robert Shaw,
Peter Willes, Jimmy Wax.

They all rang.
Or sent flowers.

1999

[IV]

The US Elephant Must Be Stopped

Guardian, 5 December 1987

In June 1986 the International Court of Justice at The Hague pronounced its judgment on the merits in the case concerning military and paramilitary activities in and against Nicaragua brought by Nicaragua against the US.

The court decided that the US, by training, arming, equipping, financing and supplying the Contra force, or otherwise encouraging, supporting and aiding military activities in and against Nicaragua, had breached its obligations under international law not to intervene in the affairs of another state.

The court decided that the US was under a duty to cease and refrain from all such acts which breach these legal obligations and make reparation for all injury caused. It recalled to both parties their obligation to seek a peaceful solution to their disputes in accordance with international law.

Unfortunately, one of the parties had long shown that it had little respect for international law. In 1965 President Lyndon Johnson said to the Greek ambassador to the US: 'Fuck your Parliament and your constitution. America is an elephant. Cyprus is a flea. Greece is a flea. If these two fellows continue itching the elephant, they may just get whacked by the elephant's trunk, whacked good . . . If your prime minister gives me talk about democracy, Parliament and constitution, he, his Parliament and his constitution may not last very long.'

He meant what he said. Two years later, the Colonels took over and the Greek people spent seven years in hell.

You have to hand it to Johnson. He sometimes told the truth, however brutal. Reagan tells lies. His celebrated description of Nicaragua as a 'totalitarian dungeon' was a lie from every conceivable angle. It was an assertion unsupported by facts; it had no basis in reality. But it's a good, vivid, resonant phrase which persuaded the unthinking with no trouble at all and, furthermore, acted as a smokescreen over the real 'totalitarian dungeons' of the time: Guatemala and El Salvador.

The facts are these, as some people know, but as others (including the British Government apparently) don't: the Nicaraguan revolution was a popular revolution which (at the cost of 50,000 dead) overthrew a dictatorship which had been supported by the US for forty years. In 1981 free elections were held – attested as such by seventy-nine observers from all over the world, including an all-party British parliamentary group.

The Sandinista government inherited a country with no organized health service, very high levels of child mortality and malnutrition, widespread illiteracy; the majority of the population poverty-stricken. The strides the new Nicaragua, despite all its obvious difficulties, has made in health and literacy are unprecedented in the region. Torture, monitored by Amnesty International and confirmed by them to be widespread and systematic in the majority of Latin American states, is not practised.

Nicaragua is a Catholic country. Three priests are government ministers. In the US attempt to define the Sandinistas as 'Marxist-Leninist anti-religious devils', it has failed to note that, of the hundreds of priests killed in Central America in the last ten years, not one died in Nicaragua.

Nicaragua is intent on establishing a decent, sane and civilized society, if left to itself. The US is not leaving it to itself but is doing its best to destroy it. Why?

The situation in Central America is not about the Kremlin's wicked ambitions – it's about money and power; about poverty, injustice, deprivation, slavery. The US has always protected its interests in the area quite rigorously. It has supported – and in some cases created – all military or rightwing dictatorships on the continent. Among other verified acts, the CIA brought down the legally elected democracies of Guatemala in 1951 and of Chile in 1973. The tortured of Latin America have been tortured for 'freedom', 'Christian principles', 'the fight against Communism'. The initials CIA may have become an exhausted cliché – good for a laugh – but the dead are not laughing.

The US dismissed the judgment of the International Court, declaring, in so many words, that its actions were none of the business of any damn International Court of Justice, although it didn't quite have the nerve to call the court a flea.

The US has done enormous and far-reaching damage to this proud, small, vulnerable and infinitely courageous country. Thousands of Nicaraguan men, women and children have been murdered and mutilated by the Contras – who Reagan compares to the Founding Fathers. They have been raped, skinned, beheaded, castrated. We have to stop the American elephant.

Eroding the Language of Freedom

We've assumed that we live in a free country for so long that it's very hard for us to subject that concept to any real or practical scrutiny. An entire range of encroachments on fundamental freedoms is taking place now in this country. It's quite a range, far-reaching and quite pernicious.

I believe that the root cause of this state of affairs is that for the last forty years our thought has been trapped in hollow structures of language, a stale, dead but immensely successful rhetoric. This has represented, in my view, a defeat of the intelligence and of the will. When the Czech police use their truncheons in Wenceslas Square, we describe that as an act of brutal repression consistent with the practices of a totalitarian regime. When the English police charge students on horseback on Westminster Bridge we describe this as a maintenance of law and order and are advised that it is a containment of essentially subversive forces. The Czechs use precisely the same language (as of course do the Turks, the Chileans, the South Africans, etc.): the demonstrations are against the state and must be crushed. Here, as there, I believe we must assess a governing power not by what it says it is, or by what it says it intends, but by what it *does*. It can call itself what it likes. In January 1986 a young woman protesting against nuclear weapons (they still do that, you know) had her finger torn off by a security guard as he yanked her from the barbed wire. This didn't happen in Czechoslovakia. It happened here.

Does Mrs Thatcher *know* what she's doing when she exhorts the Polish authorities to allow free trade unions while at exactly the same time she is firing the last trade union members here at GCHQ? Does she know what she's saying when she assures us that Prime Minister Ozal of Turkey is a man in whom she has absolute trust with reference to his respect for human rights in that country (infinitely the worst human rights record in the whole of Europe)? I take it she does, because the British got the contract to build the third bridge over the Bosporus.

Because language is discredited and because spirit and moral intelligence are fatally undermined, the government possesses carte blanche to do what it likes. Its officers can bug, break in, tap, burgle, lie, slander, bully and terrorize with impunity. Disclosure of these things will land the discloser in prison, while the government servant remains above the law, accountable neither to the citizens of this country nor to its representatives in Parliament. (The security services have of course always been above the law but this is now being given sanctity in law, so to speak.)

The laws are brutal and cynical. None of them has to do with democratic aspirations. All of them have to do with intensification and consolidation of state power. Unless we face that reality fairly and squarely, this free country is in grave danger of being strangled to death.

Sanity, March 1989

Oh, Superman

Broadcast for *Opinion*, Channel 4, 31 May 1990

Earlier this year I was in Prague and found an extraordinary state of affairs: an excited and nervous sense of disbelief, a sense of thought suddenly and shockingly embodied in action, almost a sense of the miraculous. The Czechs had freed themselves from oppression. The sense of liberation was palpable.

How did the new democratic spirit manifest itself? What was immediately evident was that a startlingly fresh environment was being created – an environment where independent, critical and open debate could flourish, and where constraint and suppression of thought was no longer acceptable.

The only other country where I've experienced anything like the same sense of spontaneity, vitality and excited if precarious endeavour was Nicaragua, when I was there in 1988. And they had been fighting a war for seven years.

When the remarkable chain of events unfolded in Eastern Europe, the world rejoiced. I'd like to look here at Central America, where the people have always had precisely the same aspirations as those of Eastern Europe: to free themselves from oppression.

The Economist, a magazine with worldwide circulation, published a leader in February of this year entitled 'Yes: You are the Superpower'. It stated that only the United States now qualifies as a Superpower and went on to say that America's role is to help other countries make the world a safer, richer place. The leader ended with the following paragraph:

A modern Superpower must be a place that lesser fry admire, even envy. The past twelve months have seen the triumph of Western ideals, of democracy and market capitalism. One of the main reasons for that triumph was that in the post-war decades,

America lived up to its ideals while Marxist beliefs turned to venal reality. America at home has to stay a land of opportunity and openness, to better ensure that the rest of the world keeps going that way. Over to you, Superman.

What the view of the 40 million Americans, living on or under the poverty line, would be of these remarks, is anyone's guess.

The USA has had a long and rigorously possessive relationship with the countries of Central America and the Caribbean basin and a particularly active one with Nicaragua.

In 1823 President Monroe declared that interference by any European power in newly emerging Latin American republics would be considered an unfriendly act towards the US itself. The 'Monroe Doctrine' established the right to 'protect' Latin America, and by the early twentieth century the US was firmly established as an imperial power in the region, prepared to back up its authority and protect its interests with brute force.

US marines occupied Nicaragua from 1912 to 1925. They took a year out and returned in 1926, 'to protect American lives and property'. But Augusto César Sandino was in the mountains with a guerrilla force and 4,000 marines failed to destroy that force. In 1927 Sandino was asked by a US marine captain to surrender. He replied, 'I have received and understood your communication of yesterday. I will not surrender and I await you here. I want a free country or death. I am not afraid of you.'

In 1933 the US finally withdrew from Nicaragua. But not before it had created, trained and equipped a constabulary army – the National Guard – under the sole command of Anastasio Somoza – who subsequently became president. Sandino was invited to Managua in 1934 to discuss disarmament with Somoza. He went in good faith. Somoza shook his hand. He left Somoza's residence. A short time later, his car was stopped. He was taken out, stood against a wall and shot.

So started the Somoza regime: a dynasty approaching royalty. It held power for over forty years, fully supported by the United States. It may have been a vicious and brutal dictatorship, but it was very good for business.

The Nicaraguan people, led by the Sandinistas, overthrew this regime in 1979 – a breathtaking, popular revolution. The US considered this an impertinent act and under President Reagan set out to destroy the perpetrators.

The 'crime' of the Sandinistas was twofold:

1. They asserted their country's independence from US influence, actually insisting on self-determination (like Czechoslovakia).

2. They set a very bad example to the region: if Nicaragua was allowed to establish basic norms of social and economic justice, if it was allowed to raise the standards of health care and education and achieve social unity and national self respect, neighbouring countries (where US multinationals and banks have vital interests) would be undermined, i.e. they might start asking the same questions and doing the same things. *My* power would be in peril – *yours* (the people of Central America) would become dangerously alive, not helpful to my best interests. Therefore you must be crushed.

The Sandinistas set out to establish a stable and decent society. The death penalty was abolished. Over 100,000 families were given title to land; more than 2,000 new schools were built; illiteracy was cut to less than one seventh. Malaria was halved; measles, tetanus and diarrhoea were dramatically reduced. Infant mortality was reduced by a third. Polio was eradicated.

The United States denounced these achievements as Marxist-Leninist subversion. It organized the Contras – a force constituted in the main by members of the old Somoza National Guard. Their policy was not to tangle with the Sandinista army but to create as much chaos as possible, to attack health centres, farms, hospitals, schools, to kill and mutilate as many women and children as they could lay their hands on; to terrorize. These tactics were cheerfully recommended at the time in a manual of terrorism written and distributed by the CIA. It was not, therefore, in any way a random policy – the Contras weren't a bunch of soccer hooligans – but a quite precise and systematic policy, inspired by the United States and financed by it.

The US went on to establish a trade blockade and financial embargo on Nicaragua. It instructed the World Bank and the IMF to cut all aid to the country. It exerted enormous pressure on Western European countries to do the same.

In 1984, despite the escalating Contra war and the consequent weakening of the economy (50 per cent of the national budget now spent on defence), the Sandinistas called an election. This was recognized as a free and democratic election by observers from all over the world, including an all-party British parliamentary delegation. The United States drew one of the main opposition parties out of the election, hoping by these means to render the results null and void. This stratagem failed. Eighty per cent of the electorate voted. No trace of fraud or manipulation was found. The Sandinistas won 67 per cent of the vote.

On the day the election results were announced, emergency news flashes flashed across the screens of American television. The flashes said 'MiGs to Nicaragua'. This was a brilliant propaganda coup. The election results were totally obscured. 'The Russians are sending MiGs to Nicaragua! We're about to be under attack!' The Russians were not, of course, sending MiGs to Nicaragua. And the Sandinistas did not invade Texas.

In February 1985 Mrs Thatcher said in Parliament, 'Vice President Ramirez called on me. I made it clear that the Government's future relations with Nicaragua would be determined by progress towards establishing genuine democracy there.' It seemed to have slipped her mind that the Nicaraguans had just held democratic elections. The truth is that this fact was ignored for years by both the American and the British media. Why? Perhaps it was not considered to be in the public interest.

It was more dramatic to refer to Nicaragua as a Marxist-Leninist totalitarian dungeon. And that's what President Reagan did. He did it, in fact, until he was blue in the face. It's easy, vivid rhetoric, all too easily believed. Reagan also made the following comparison: 'The Contras are the moral equivalent of our Founding Fathers and of the brave men and women of the French resistance.' An unarmed Sandinista union official was captured by the Contras last year. They broke his limbs, cut off his lips and tongue, gouged out his eyes and castrated him. This is a classic Contra technique, executed many many times in Nicaragua. It's fully in accordance with death squad procedures in El Salvador and Guatemala and entirely consistent with the methods the United States encourages to keep Central America clean for democracy. I think the Founding Fathers would be slightly surprised to read this description of their moral standing.

Why was the United States doing all this? Why was it trying to bring an already poverty-stricken country to its knees, to bleed it to death? The US itself reiterated the following assertion: 'We want Nicaragua to return to democracy.' Return to democracy meant of course, in this case, a return to something like the Somoza regime, a return to dictatorship. The United States has always been very comfortable with friendly dictatorships. They've created and supported enough of them. They've had extremely happy relationships with the dictatorships in Haiti, in Chile, in Guatemala, in Paraguay, and the military dictatorships of Argentina, Uruguay and Brazil in their long and appalling periods of power could always rely on the warm and full support of the United States.

So the one country in the whole of the Central American region which had held democratic elections five years after it overthrew a dictatorship is itself accused of being a dictatorship, in comparison to its neighbours which are, in fact, military dictatorships but which are described as democracies. This is language standing on its head.

The relationship of the USA to its friendly dictators follows a classic pattern. You set him up, you construct his torture chambers, you send in your experts and your advisors, he kills as many thousands of people as you both think necessary, the people are subdued and now everything is fine. There's a stable society, a stable economy and you can do business. This state of affairs prevails for a few years. Then the dictator starts to irritate you. He gets too big for his boots. He doesn't do exactly what he's told. He's found to be a drug dealer. (What a surprise.) He begins to give you a bad name. So you destabilize him, you get rid of him. In the case of Panama, of course, you go in yourself and get him. And while you're getting him you manage to kill about a thousand innocent people. You pretend it's two hundred, and even if it had been two hundred, it would have been two hundred innocent people, but in Panama City it was a thousand which you simply call two hundred. And you say, 'We're doing this because we believe in democracy.'

What should be remembered is that the United States has never been very much concerned with 'moral considerations'. They're regarded as kind of sissy. The US believes in *action* and it takes that action as it sees fit.

The terms used to justify such action are broad and simple: 'We are protecting Christianity against Communism.' I always thought it quite ironic that there were three priests in the Sandinista government; two Jesuits (the Minister of Culture and the Minister of Education) and a Maryknoll missionary (the Foreign Minister). The Americans were never able to get the hang of this. It didn't quite make sense. After all, this was supposed to be a Marxist-Leninist totalitarian dictatorship. Therefore atheistic, surely, since you can't be a Marxist-Leninist totalitarian without being an atheist, can you? So what were three priests doing in the government?

Also, there seems to be no record of the Sandinistas ever killing a priest.

They do that in El Salvador. The assassination of Archbishop Romero in 1980 – the vicious murder of the six Jesuits at the Central American University in 1989 – stands out among the dozens upon dozens of priests tortured and killed in El Salvador over the last twenty years. The US gives the El Salvadorean army over a million dollars a day to defend Christianity against this dangerous pack of Marxist-Leninist Jesuit atheists.

If you spew out lie after lie day after day, even the liar becomes convinced he is telling the truth. Or does he? The Reagan administration was in the habit of making constant references to something called the Sandinistas' human rights record. It became a chant; it was a proposition never questioned. The truth is that the Sandinistas' human rights record was infinitely the most dignified, serious and responsible in the whole of the region – with the possible exception of Costa Rica.

There is no record of death squads under the Sandinista government. There is no record of torture. There is no record of systematic or official military brutality. There were certainly sporadic bursts of military revenge against the Contra atrocities, which were recognized by the authorities as crimes and dealt with according to the law.

Compare this with the human rights records of Guatemala and El Salvador. In Guatemala we must talk of genocide against the Indian population. Men, women and children have suffered massacres and brutal assault in almost unimaginable ways to the tune of 160,000 dead and disappeared over the last twenty years. In El Salvador exactly the same state of affairs obtains. The record there is between 70,000 and 80,000 dead over the same period. In Nicaragua the Contra war resulted in well over 30,000 people dead and over 5,000 maimed for life. A goodly proportion of these people were raped, skinned, beheaded, ripped open. President Bush made no mention of them when he congratulated Mrs Chamorro on her victory. Hardly anybody has bothered to mention them at all.

So in this little region of Central America nearly 300,000 people have been killed in the name of freedom and democracy over the last twenty years. Now let's be quite clear about why they were killed – they were killed because they were a nuisance. They were killed because they believed in a better life for all. That belief immediately qualified them as Communists. It's very odd and terribly ironic that while the Communist system in Eastern Europe has been collapsing and everyone's been saying that Communism is dead, the Americans remain unconvinced. In Washington they still take the view that there are plenty of Communists left in Latin America and they consider that they don't deserve to live. Who are these people? The poor, of course – priests, health workers, doctors, trade union members, reporters, students, teachers, poets, people working with human rights organizations. They're a danger to a stable society, they're a danger to the orderly conduct of business. Even if you're not inclined to kill them, you certainly don't help them. The British Government, for example, gave not an inch of any kind of aid, not an inch of any kind of recognition to Nicaragua – just the barest diplomatic nod, grudgingly accepting it as a bone fide country. So that when, for example, the terrible hurricane hit the country in October 1988 Great Britain gave a mere £250,000 in aid. The US gave nothing. It was clearly a Communist hurricane.

The US has naturally welcomed the efforts of the East European countries toward self-determination. Everyone was horrified when the Russians invaded Czechoslovakia in 1968. But what Washington has done to Nicaragua is exactly what Moscow did to Czechoslovakia in 1968, but the US has done it by different means. Instead of tanks, it destroyed the health service and ruined the economy and frightened the populace. So the electorate had to balance life and liberty against hunger and death. And hunger and death won.

As for the United States, what will it do now? The trouble,

it seems to me, is that the United States was really turned on by the idea of Soviet aggression. It justified everything. It was there with the cornflakes every morning. It was part of the American way of life. You had an enemy and you loved him. You had a knife at his belly but you hugged him to you because he was your lover in death. You needed him. You were talking about death. All your references were to do with death. But you were happy. It was a good time. You could go all over the world and help your friends torture and kill other people – journalists, teachers, students, peasants, etc. – because these people, you said, were part of *them*. They were inspired by *them*, they were corrupted by *them*. And by forever talking about *them*, you conserved and tightened your own power. But if that's all over, what are you going to do? If you no longer have a good fat enemy, if you can no longer spend billions of dollars on armaments and *make* billions of dollars from armaments; what the hell do you do? What happens when there is no more Soviet aggression? What happens when the Soviet Union says, as it appears to be doing, 'We no longer want to be a Superpower, we no longer *are* a Superpower'? What does poor old America do then? Because America loves being a Superpower – it simply does.

Carlos Fuentes has said that the Soviet Union is dispensing with its useless ideological baggage while the United States insists on dealing with the world only in ideological terms. Is it possible that the US view of the world might change? There seems little evidence to support such a hope.

I suggest that US foreign policy can still be defined as 'kiss my ass or I'll kick your head in'. But of course it doesn't put it like that. It talks of 'low intensity conflict'. What that actually means is that you put a few mines in a harbour – which the CIA did in Nicaragua – and then deny that they've anything to do with you. They must have fallen off the back of a lorry. When you're brought up before the International Court of Justice in The Hague in 1986, which finds you guilty on *eight counts* of violating International Law and asks you not only to cease your aggression against Nicaragua but to make reparations for the damage you have caused, you simply toss your head and say that the matter is outside the province of the International Court. Low intensity conflict means that thousands of people die, but slower than if you dropped a bomb on the lot of them at one fell swoop. It means that you infect the heart of a country, that you establish a malignant growth and you watch the gangrene bloom. And then you go in front of the cameras in a clean shirt and a nice tie and you say that democracy has prevailed.

What all this adds up to is a disease at the very centre of language, so that language becomes a permanent masquerade, a tapestry of lies. The ruthless and cynical mutilation and degradation of human beings, both in spirit and body, the death of countless thousands – these actions are justified by rhetorical gambits, sterile terminology and concepts of power which stink. Are we ever going to look at the language we use, I wonder? Is it within our capabilities to do so?

Do the structures of language and the structures of reality (by which I mean what actually *happens*) move along parallel lines? Does reality essentially remain outside language, separate, obdurate, alien, not susceptible to description? Is an accurate and vital correspondence between what *is* and our perception of it impossible? Or is it that we are obliged to use language only in order to obscure and distort reality – to distort what *is*, to distort what *happens* – because we fear it? We are encouraged to be cowards. We can't face the dead. But we must face the dead because they die in our name. We must pay attention to what is being done in our name. I believe it's because of the way we use language that we have got ourselves into this terrible trap, where words like freedom, democracy and Christian values are still used to justify barbaric and shameful policies and acts. We are under a serious and urgent obligation to subject such terms to an intense critical scrutiny. If we fail to do so, both our moral and political judgement will remain fatally impaired.

[213]

Blowing up the Media

American Football (A Reflection upon the Gulf War)

Hallelujah!
It works.
We blew the shit out of them.

We blew the shit right back up their own ass
And out their fucking ears.

It works.
We blew the shit out of them.
They suffocated in their own shit!

Hallelujah.
Praise the Lord for all good things.

We blew them into fucking shit.
They are eating it.

Praise the Lord for all good things.

We blew their balls into shards of dust,
Into shards of fucking dust.

We did it.

Now I want you to come over here and kiss me on the mouth.

I started to write this poem on the plane going to the Edinburgh Festival in August 1991. I had a rough draft by the time we landed in Edinburgh. It sprang from the triumphalism, the *machismo*, the victory parades, that were very much in evidence at the time. So that is the reason for 'We blew the shit out of them.' The first place I sent it to was the *London Review of Books*. I received a very odd letter, which said, in sum, that the poem had considerable force, but it was for that very reason that they were not able to publish it. But the letter went on to make the extraordinary assertion that the paper shared my views about the USA's role in the world.

So I wrote back. 'The paper shares my views, does it? I'd keep that to myself if I were you, chum,' I said. And I was very pleased with the use of the word 'chum'.

So I sent it to the *Guardian* and the then literary editor came on the telephone to me and said, 'Oh dear.' He said, 'Harold, this is really ... You've really given me a very bad headache with this one.' He said, 'I'm entirely behind you myself, speaking personally.' This is my memory of the telephone conversation. 'But,' he said, 'you know I don't think ... Oooh, I think we're in for real trouble if we try to publish it in the *Guardian*.' Really, I asked innocently, why is that?

He said, 'Well, you know, Harold, we are a family newspaper.' Those words were actually said. 'Oh, I'm sorry,' I said, 'I was under the impression you were a serious newspaper.' And he said, 'Well, yes, we're also a serious newspaper, of course. Nevertheless things have changed a bit in the *Guardian* over the last few years.'

I suggested he talk to some of his colleagues and come back to me in a couple of days. Because, I said, 'I do believe the *Guardian* has a responsibility to publish serious work, seriously considered work, which I believe this to be. Although it is very hot, I also think it is steely. Hot steel ...'

He called me in two days and said, 'Harold, I'm terribly sorry, I can't publish it.' He more or less said, It's more than my job's worth. So that was the *Guardian*. I then sent it to the *Observer*.

The *Observer* was the most complex and fascinating web that I actually ran into. I sent the poem not to the literary editor, but to the editor himself.

A couple of days later, he called me and said that he thought it should be published. He thought it was very testing. Probably going to be quite a lot of flack, he said. But he thought it should be published, not on the literary pages, but on the leader page. It was a truly political poem, he said. So I was delighted to hear that. He'd send me a proof, which he did.

The next Sunday nothing happened. And then the following Sunday nothing happened. So I called the editor. He said, 'Oh dear, Harold, I'm afraid that I've run into one or two problems with your poem.' I asked what they were. 'In short, my colleagues don't want me to publish it.' Why not? He said, 'They're telling me we are going to lose lots of readers.' I asked, Do you really believe that? Anyway, we had a quite amiable chat. He said, 'I want to publish it but I seem to be more or less alone.' I then said, Look, the *Observer*, as a serious newspaper, has in fact published quite recently an account of what the US tanks actually did in the desert. The tanks had bulldozers, and during the ground attack they were used as sweepers. They buried, as far as we know, an untold number of Iraqis alive. This was reported by your newspaper as a fact and it was a horrific and obscene fact. My poem actually says, 'They suffocated in their own shit.' It is obscene, but it is referring to obscene facts.

He said, 'Absolutely right. Look, I want to publish the poem. But I'm running into all sorts of resistance. The trouble is the language, it's the obscene language. People get very offended by this and that's why they think we are going to lose readers.' I then sent the editor of the *Observer* a short fax, in which I quoted myself when I was at the US Embassy in Ankara in March 1985 with Arthur Miller. I had a chat with the ambassador about torture in Turkish prisons. He told me that I didn't appreciate the realities of the situation vis-à-vis the Communist threat, the military reality, the diplomatic reality, the strategic reality, and so on.

I said the reality I was referring to was that of electric current on your genitals. Whereupon the ambassador said, 'Sir, you are a guest in my house,' and turned away. I left the house.

The point I was making to the editor of the *Observer* was that the ambassador found great offence in the word genitals. But the reality of the situation, the actual reality of electric current on your genitals, was a matter of no concern to him. It was the use of the *word* that was offensive, but not the act. I said I was drawing an analogy between that little exchange, and what we were now talking about. This poem uses obscene words to describe obscene acts and obscene attitudes.

But the editor of the *Observer* wrote to me and said he couldn't publish, with great regret. 'I've been giving serious thought to publication of your poem on the Gulf War. As you know, my first instinct was in favour, despite warnings by senior colleagues that many readers would be offended . . . I admit to having cold feet.'

Recently an *Observer* columnist spoke of his paper's rejection of the poem and referred to his editor's concern 'for its shortcomings as a piece of verse'. But nobody ever said, 'We don't think this poem is good enough. It is not a successful piece of work.' Nobody has actually said that.

I then sent the poem to the literary editor of the *Independent*, saying I hadn't sent it to him in the first place because I did not think the *Independent* would publish it. But now that everybody had turned it down, the *London Review of Books*, the *Guardian* and the *Observer*, perhaps I was wrong about the *Independent*! To cut a long story very short, the literary editor wanted to publish it but he felt he had to show it to the editor. The editor sat on it for a few days and then made no comment except to say the *Independent* was not going to publish the poem. And I've never had any explanation. Nothing. It was simply No.

I did send it to the *New York Review of Books*, just as a laugh. The editor thanked me warmly for sending the poem, but said he was afraid they couldn't use it. So I did not waste any more time. I heard that a magazine called *Bomb*, a very well-produced publication in the West Village, might be interested, and indeed they published the poem.

It was finally published in Britain, in January 1992, by a new newspaper called *Socialist*, with a limited circulation. But as far as national newspapers go, in Holland it was published in one of the main Dutch dailies, *Handelsblad* – in no uncertain terms, too, with an article written by the editor about the rejection in England. And it was published in Bulgaria, Greece and Finland.

Index on Censorship, May 1992

The US and El Salvador

Seventy-five thousand dead in El Salvador over the last fifteen years. Who killed them and who cares?

Hugh O'Shaughnessy, in last Sunday's *Observer*, reported the findings of the UN Truth Commission set up to investigate the slaughter. (No other British newspaper thought these findings worth more than the most cursory mention.)

The UN Commission declared that the vast majority of human rights abuses were committed by the Salvadorean armed forces rather than the FMLN guerrillas. The Commission not only named army officers but ministers in Government as guilty parties and recommended that they be banned from public and military service forthwith. It also called for the mass resignation of the Supreme Court. President Alfredo Cristiani's response to this was to force through the legislative assembly an amnesty for all the accused. They will face no criminal charges. They are absolved. They are free men.

The people killed included social workers, students, priests, trade union officials, doctors, nurses, journalists, human rights activists, school teachers and, of course, thousands upon thousands of peasants. But the armed forces, if they did well, were sometimes offered some especially juicy prizes. Ripping a few thousand illiterate peasants to death can become a mundane pastime, but shooting Archbishop Romero while he's saying mass, and killing six of the most distinguished Jesuits in the world in one fell swoop, mean that among your colleagues you become a star overnight. That blood is glamorous blood.

But who did the offering? Who guided and advised the soldiers in their endeavours? Who nurtured them?

José Maria Tojeira, the present Rector of the Central American University (where the Jesuits were killed) said that William Walker, the US ambassador in San Salvador at the time of the massacres, 'in some way knew what was going on and hindered the investigation'. A human rights worker added: 'The US is the missing protagonist in this case.'

It sure is.

The United States subsidized the Salvadorean government to the tune of $6 billion throughout the 1980s. But it did far more than subsidize one of the most brutal military dictatorships of the twentieth century. It was a very active involvement indeed.

It has now been established that half an hour before the Jesuits were murdered, President Cristiani attended a Salvadorean army briefing at which two or three US officers were also present. This is no great surprise. There were plenty of US officers present throughout the whole enterprise. They were known as 'advisers', experts in the field.

Their 'field' ranged from a strategic concept which applied to the whole of Central America down to more specific and precise recommendations. These included the most efficient methods of skinning alive, castration and disembowelment. These techniques, one is led to understand, were employed in order to defend Christianity and democracy against the Devil.

Under President Cristiani's amnesty, not only the named army officers and government ministers will walk free, but also two soldiers now in prison for the murder of the Jesuits and five imprisoned for the rape and murder of four American churchwomen in 1980. But there is another and quite substantial body of people which also walks free, indeed has not been charged. This body includes the American 'military advisers', the CIA, Elliot Abrams, former head of the US Latin American Desk, Jeanne Kirkpatrick, former US ambassador to the United Nations, former Secretary of State Al Haig, and ex-Presidents Reagan and Bush.

Members of the US Congress and correspondents in the American press are evidently dismayed at the disclosure of the extent of American involvement in the nefarious operations of the Salvadorean government. It seems to have taken them quite by surprise. They apparently knew nothing about it until the UN Commission report was published. Information of this sort is, of course, notoriously hard to come by.

However, if a congressional investigation actually takes place, what might it bring about? The answer is nothing. There is one good reason for this. The US has long assumed a position as the world's moral centre, the world's 'Dad'. This is so deeply embedded in official American thinking that to tear this assumption apart would be to perform an operation without anaesthetic. The US Congress and media would, I believe, find this insupportable.

Anyway, in this 'post-Communist world' where 'real values' are prevailing and free-market forces are operating so happily, it is perfectly reasonable to consign the mistakes of our past to the past and bury them.

Why did these people in El Salvador die? They died because in one way or another or to one degree or another they dared to question the status quo, the endless plateau of poverty, disease, degradation and oppression which is their birthright. On behalf of the dead, we must regard the breathtaking discrepancy between US government language and US government action with the absolute contempt it merits.

The US has done really well since the end of the Second World War. It has exercised a sustained, systematic, remorseless and quite clinical manipulation of power worldwide, while masquerading as 'a force for universal good'. It's a brilliant, even witty, certainly highly successful con-job. But it's really about time the gaff was blown and the real tale told. Perhaps the new President of the United States will do it.

Observer, 28 March 1993

Pinter: Too Rude for Convicts

by Alan Travis, Home Affairs Editor, *Guardian*,
9 June 1995

A prison governor has banned performances of three Harold Pinter plays in his jail because they contain too much bad language and the subject matter of one of them was said to be unsuitable for convicted criminals.

The decision has led to the resignation of part-time drama teacher, Christopher Davies, from his job at Ashwell Prison, near Oakham, Leicestershire, after three years. He claims he was told by one senior official that the performances were being cancelled because the three short plays – *Mountain Language, One for the Road* and *Victoria Station* – were not well written and had no entertainment value.

A Prison Service statement said yesterday: 'The governor of Ashwell prison took the decision to stop rehearsals because of the unsuitable subject matter of one of the plays, which included torture, rape and child murder.'

In a letter to Mr Davies, accepting his resignation, Ashwell's governor, Henry Reid, said there was too much bad language and explicit sexual innuendo in the plays and the subjects of torture, rape and child murder dealt with in *One for the Road* were not best suited to 'preparing inmates for a good and useful life on release'.

Mr Davies, who has put on plays at the prison for the past three years, said: 'The reason seems to be that the governor won't have strong language used in his prison. All the three plays use the "F-word" but it is not out of place in the context.'

He said the objections to the subject matter of *One for the Road* were absurd: 'The play is about interrogation. It only refers to the subjects of murder, rape and torture in an off-stage way. There is no portrayal of violence on stage.'

Mr Davies said he had heard far worse language used by inmates in the audience at a performance of a pantomime at the prison.

Mr Reid insisted that there had been an 'error of judgement' and said the prison authorities had only taken a closer look at the programme when some of the inmates stated they would feel uncomfortable performing the plays in front of an audience.

Caribbean Cold War

So Clinton has signed the Helms/Burton bill, citing Cuba's 'scorn for international law'. What a joke. In the course of its endeavours to keep the world safe for democracy the US has broken international law more times than I've had hot dinners, and done it with impunity.

Even the poor old United Nations has condemned the US trade embargo of Cuba by an overwhelming majority for three years running (1993–5: 88–4, 101–2 and 117–3) and been totally ignored by the convicted party. This is perhaps why the British, Canadian and Mexican governments don't propose a motion to the Security Council condemning this further legislation which sets out to prevent free trade between Cuba and the rest of the world in terms which are in blatant breach of the UN Charter and the aforesaid international law. They've probably worked out that it would be like farting 'Annie Laurie' down a keyhole, as we used to say in the good old days. Be that as it may, the truth is plain: this is an exercise of arrogant power which stinks.

The most astonishing thing about Cuba is quite simply that it has survived. After over thirty-five years of the most ruthless economic violence, thirty-five years of unremitting and virulent hostility from the US, Cuba remains an independent sovereign state. This is a quite remarkable achievement. Not many states have remained independent or 'sovereign' for long in the US 'backyard'.

Here are three short extracts from Duncan Green's book *Silent Revolution*. This is the first, describing delegates of the World Bank at dinner:

The dinner was catered by Ridgewells at $200 per person. Guests began with crab cakes, caviar, crème fraîche, smoked salmon and mini beef wellingtons. The fish course was lobster with corn rounds followed by citrus sorbet. The entrée was duck with lime sauce served with artichoke bottoms filled with baby carrots. A hearts of palm salad was offered accompanied by sage cheese soufflés with a port wine dressing. Dessert was a German chocolate turnip sauced with raspberry coulis, ice cream bon bons and flaming coffee royale.

The wine list isn't mentioned.

Here is the second extract:

The tiny adobe house is crammed with gnarled Bolivian mining women in patched shawls and battered felt hats, whose calloused hands work breaking up rocks on the surface in search of scraps of tin ore. The paths between the miners' huts are strewn with plastic bags and human excrement, dried black in the sun.

This is a Bolivian woman speaking:

In the old days women used to stay at home because the men had work. Now we have to work. Many of our children have been abandoned. Their fathers have left and there's no love left in us when we get home late from work. We leave food for them. They play in the streets. There are always accidents and no doctors. I feel like a slave in my own country. We get up at 4 a.m. and at 11 at night we are still working. I have vomited blood for weeks at a time and still had to keep working.

No doubt after dinner the World Bank delegates discussed the Bolivian economy and made their recommendations.

This monstrous inequality is precisely what inspired the Cuban revolution. The revolution set out to correct such grotesque polarization and was determined to ensure that the Cuban people would never have to endure such degradation again.

It understood that recognition of and respect for human dignity were crucial obligations which devolved upon a civilized society. Its achievements are remarkable. It constructed a health service which can hardly be rivalled and established an extraordinary level of literacy. All this the US found to be abominable Marxist-Leninist subversion and naturally set out to destroy it. It has failed. And it must be true to say that Cuba could never have survived unless it possessed a formidable centre of pride, faith and solidarity.

There is the question of human rights. I don't believe in the relativity of human rights. I don't believe that 'local conditions', as it were, or a specific cultural disposition can justify suppression of dissent or the individual conscience. In Cuba I have always understood harsh treatment of dissenting voices as stemming from a 'siege situation' imposed upon it from outside. And I believe that to a certain extent that is true. But equally apologists for Israeli actions have also stressed a siege situation brought about by external threat. Mordechai Vanunu is a dissenting voice in Israel and was sentenced to eighteen years' solitary confinement for disclosing Israel's nuclear capacity to the world.

I am a trustee of the Vanunu estate and a defender of his right to speak. I must therefore logically defend, for example, Maria Elena Cruz Varela's right to speak also. Socialism must be about active and participatory debate.

However, the wrinkled moral frown of the US has always been good for a laugh. 'We deplore, etc., etc., the violations of human rights in such and such a country.' In their own country one and a half million people are in jail, 3,000 are on Death Row, nearly fifty million live under the poverty line, effectively disenfranchised, there is a huge black underclass, abused and condemned, thirty-eight states practise the death penalty, corruption is vibrant and active at all levels of the hierarchy, police brutality is systematic, heavily racist, lethal. Human rights, where are you?

There exists today widespread propaganda which asserts that socialism is dead. But if to be a socialist is to be a person convinced that the words 'the common good' and 'social justice' actually mean something; if to be a socialist is to be outraged at the contempt in which millions and millions of people are held by those in power, by 'market forces', by international financial institutions; if to be a socialist is to be a person determined to do everything in his or her power to alleviate these unforgivably degraded lives, then socialism can never be dead because these aspirations will never die.

Red Pepper, May 1996

Mountain Language in Haringey

by Duncan Campbell, *Guardian*, 21 June 1996

OFFICER: Now hear this. You are mountain people. You hear me?
... It is not permitted to speak your mountain language in this
place ... It is outlawed. You may only speak the language of the
capital ... You will be badly punished if you attempt to speak your
mountain language in this place. This is a military decree ... Any
questions?

Mountain Language by Harold Pinter

Armed men in uniform. Hooded hostages held at gunpoint.
Automatic weapons. It seemed the stuff of urban nightmare.

When a concerned resident of Haringey, north London,
spotted a group of armed and uniformed men entering the
local Kurdish community centre, the police responded in
numbers.

Officers sped to the scene in Portland Gardens. Police
marksmen stationed themselves on rooftops with automatic
weapons trained on entrances and exits. A helicopter was
dispatched. Tension mounted.

Those emerging from the hall were told to put their hands
up, grabbed, handcuffed, and forbidden to communicate with
one another in Kurdish or Turkish. Finally, after an hour,
doors were smashed, and police entered the building.

Inside were the remaining props and scripts used by the
Kurdish actors from the Yeni Yasam (New Life) company in
a rehearsal of their production of Harold Pinter's *Mountain
Language*. No real weapons were found. End of siege.

The 25-minute play, first performed at the National Thea-
tre in 1988, is about the persecution of people who choose to
speak their own dialect. In the course of it, hooded prisoners
are interrogated and tortured.

Last night, Scotland Yard confirmed that officers had responded on Wednesday night to reports of armed men in uniform. There had been fears of a possible shoot-out between members of the Turkish and Kurdish communities, between whom relations have been volatile because of the treatment of the Kurds in Turkey.

Yesterday officers were trying to patch up doors and community relations with apologies and promises of speedy repairs.

'It was really tense and really OTT,' said the community centre's co-ordinator, Sheri Laizer. 'There were about fifty or sixty officers. People tried to explain that it was just a rehearsal of a play. We had told the local police station last Sunday about it and they said there would be no problem. We even had receipts for the plastic guns from the National, but the police wouldn't listen to anyone who was Kurdish or let them talk to each other.'

Harold Pinter, who said his play was inspired by the Kurdish situation although not specifically about the Kurds, said: 'The line between fiction and reality sometimes becomes very blurred.'

He added that he was touched that a Kurdish group was performing it and intended to see it when it reaches the stage next month at Hoxton Hall in east London.

A Pinter Drama in Stoke Newington

Letter to the *Guardian*, 9 July 1996

The armed police who raided the Stoke Newington rehearsal room where Kurdish actors were rehearsing my play *Mountain Language* (front-page report, 21 June) manhandled them, handcuffed them and forbade them to speak in their own language. The Kurds, most of them refugees, thought the police were so forceful and deaf to reason that they felt they were back in Turkey.

The production of the play itself was extremely moving, and particularly significant in that a number of the participants had themselves been imprisoned and tortured in Turkish prisons.

The appalling repression of the Kurdish people in Turkey is generally unreported in the British media and virtually ignored at government level. Vast numbers of Kurdish villages have been destroyed and their inhabitants displaced, thousands of people tortured and murdered. State terror is systematic, savage, merciless. All efforts on the part of the Kurds to bring about a political rather than military resolution to the conflict have failed. The international community shows little interest in any of this. Turkey is a member of Nato, the United States subsidizes its army to the hilt, and of course the country provides rich business opportunities for all Western 'democracies'.

Meanwhile the Kurds are persecuted beyond endurance. They are a race of immense pride, dignity and courage. Their plight desperately calls for recognition and support.

It Never Happened

Can it be true? Are the other 'major powers' in the world finally moving towards a position where their contempt for the assertion of US power is actually being embodied in action?

For the fourth year running the United Nations has voted for the motion condemning the US embargo of Cuba, this time by 137 votes (including Great Britain!) to three. The countries against the motion were the US, Israel and Uzbekistan. The European Union is taking the US to the World Trade Organization panel, arguing that the Helms/Burton bill is illegal. Fourteen out of fifteen members of the Security Council (including Great Britain!) voted against the US veto of Boutros Boutros-Ghali. The US was on its own.

How can any country stand out against such a consensus? How can any country, in the light of such blanket condemnation of its policies and actions, not pause to take a little thought, not subject itself to even the mildest and most tentative critical scrutiny? The answer is quite simple. If you believe you still call all the shots you just don't give a shit. You say, without beating about the bush: Yes, sure, I am biased and arrogant and in many respects ignorant, but so what? I possess the economic and military might to back me up to the hilt and I don't care who knows it. And when I say that I also occupy the moral high ground you'd better believe it.

The US is without doubt the greatest show on the road. Brutal, indifferent, scornful and ruthless it may be, but it's also very smart. As a salesman it's out on its own. And its most saleable commodity is self-love. It's a winner. The US has actually educated itself to be in love with itself. Listen to President Clinton – and before him, Bush and before him, Reagan and before him all the others – say on television the words 'the American People' as in the sentence, 'I say to the American People it is time to pray and to defend the rights of the American People and I ask the American People to trust their president in the action he is about to take on behalf of the American People.' A nation weeps.

It's a pretty brilliant stratagem. Language is actually employed to keep thought at bay. The words 'the American People' provide a truly voluptuous cushion of reassurance. You don't need to think. Just lie back on the cushion. The cushion may be suffocating your intelligence and your critical faculties but you don't know that. Nobody tells you. So the status quo remains where it is and Father Christmas remains American and America remains the Land of the Brave and the Home of the Free.

Except of course for the 1.5 million people in prison, the 50 million living under the poverty line, the adolescents and mentally deficient about to be gassed or injected or electrocuted in the thirty-eight out of fifty states which carry the death penalty. They don't feel quite the same about this cushion of reassurance, but nobody listens to them anyway. As they are mostly poor and black they are essentially subversive. They are subversive because where they are resentful and critical and degraded and angry they threaten the stability of the state. The one thing they can have is God. If they want him. God belongs to every American. Successive American presidents have made this quite clear.

Sometimes you look back into recent history and you ask: did all that really happen? Were half a million 'Communists' massacred in Indonesia in 1965 (the rivers clogged with corpses)? Were 200,000 people killed in East Timor in 1975 by the Indonesian invaders? Have 300,000 people died in Central America since 1960? Has the persecution of the Kurdish people in Turkey reached levels which approach genocide? Are countless Iraqi children dying every month for lack of food and medicine brought about by UN sanctions? Did the military coups in Argentina, Uruguay, Brazil and

Chile result in levels of repression and depth of suffering comparable to Nazi Germany, Stalinist Russia and the Khmer Rouge? And has the US to one degree or another inspired, engendered, subsidized and sustained all these states of affairs?

The answer is yes. It has and it does. But you wouldn't know it.

It never happened. Nothing ever happened. Even *while* it was happening it wasn't happening. It didn't matter. It was of no interest. The crimes of the US throughout the world have been systematic, constant, clinical, remorseless and fully documented but *nobody talks about them*. Nobody ever has. It's probably more than a newspaper or TV channel's life is worth to do so. And it must be said that as the absolute necessity of economic control is at the bottom of all this, any innocent bystander who raises his head must be kicked in the teeth. This is entirely logical. The market must and will overcome.

Perhaps the story that really takes the biscuit or beats the band or finally makes the cat laugh is the story of Haiti, a story virtually ignored by the world for decades. Haiti suffered under the grisly Duvalier dictatorships and their paramilitary force, the Tontons Macoutes, for twenty-nine years. By 1986 popular feeling was so powerful that the Duvalier regime collapsed. Other military dictatorships followed but in 1990 the first democratic election in Haiti took place. President Aristide was elected with 67 per cent of the vote. His platform: 'To bring the Haitian people from misery to dignity.' Eight months later there was a coup d'état. For three years the military again ruled. During this period 5,000 people were killed. The US was finally forced to act. It led a UN force to the island to 'restore democracy'.

What it actually did was to restore the status quo, to give the generals various modes of asylum and protection and to effectively emasculate Aristide. His economic policies, for which the people had elected him, were discarded. The IMF and the World Bank moved in. They insisted on the application of a structural adjustment policy which threatens all hope of equitable development and progress in the country. People in Haiti refer to this plan as the 'Death Plan'. It will destroy the country's peasant economy. As a rider, the US army took from the Haitian army headquarters 160,000 pages of documents. The US government refuses to return these documents. Why? Guess. The documents show the extent of CIA involvement in the coup which overthrew Aristide in 1991.

Lastly, an elegy. Curtains are drawn, lights go out. It's as if it never happened. In Nicaragua in 1979, the Sandinistas triumphed in a remarkable popular revolution against the Somoza dictatorship. They went on to address their poverty-stricken country with unprecedented vigour and sense of purpose. They introduced a literacy campaign and health provision for all citizens which were unheard of in the region, if not throughout the whole continent. The Sandinistas had plenty of faults but they were thoughtful, intelligent, decent and without malice. They created an active, spontaneous, pluralistic society. The US destroyed, through all means at its disposal and at the cost of 30,000 dead, the whole damn thing. And they're proud of it.

The general thrust these days is: 'Oh come on, it's all in the past, nobody's interested any more, it didn't work, that's all, everyone knows what the Americans are like, but stop being naïve, this is the world, there's nothing to be done about it and anyway, fuck it, who cares?' Sure, as they say, sure. But let me put it this way – the dead are still looking at us, steadily, waiting for us to acknowledge our part in their murder.

Guardian, 4 December 1996

Scenario for the Bugging of a Home

Letter to the Editor of *The Times*, 8 January 1997

Sir, I write with reference to the Police Bill, now passing through Parliament with no discernible opposition from Her Majesty's Opposition. Since the Bill will legalize 'bugging' of private property by the police I take it the following sequence of events is logical.

A householder discovers a police officer bugging his house. He (or she) asks the officer to remove himself and the bug. The officer refuses, arguing that his activity is entirely legal. The householder persists, arguing in turn that what is taking place is an invasion of age-old rights of privacy. The officer cautions the householder. The householder refuses to give way. He is then placed under arrest for obstructing a police officer in the course of his duty.

Would the Home Secretary confirm or deny this scenario?

An Open Letter to the Prime Minister

Guardian, 17 February 1998

Dear Prime Minister,

We have been reminded often over the last few weeks of Saddam Hussein's appalling record in the field of human rights. It is indeed appalling: brutal, pathological. But I thought you might be interested to scrutinize the record of your ally, the US, in a somewhat wider context. I am not at all certain that your advisors will have kept you fully informed.

The US has supported, subsidized and, in a number of cases, engendered every right-wing military dictatorship in the world since 1945. I refer to Guatemala, Indonesia, Chile, Greece, Uruguay, the Philippines, Brazil, Paraguay, Haiti, Turkey, El Salvador, for example. Hundreds of thousands of people have been murdered by these regimes but the money, the resources, the equipment (all kinds), the advice, the moral support, as it were, has come from successive US administrations.

The deaths really do mount up: 170,000 in Guatemala, 200,000 in East Timor, 80,000 in El Salvador, 30,000 in Nicaragua, 500,000 in Indonesia – and that's just to be going on with. They are, every single one of them, attributable to your ally's foreign policy.

The devastation the US inflicted upon Vietnam, Laos and Cambodia, the use of napalm, Agent Orange and the employment of new bombs which sprayed darts inside people's bodies and finally wrenched their guts out was a remorseless, savage, systematic course of destruction, which, however, failed to destroy the spirit of the Vietnamese people. When the US was defeated it at once set out to starve the country by way of trade embargo.

The US invaded the Dominican Republic in 1965, Grenada

in 1983, Panama in 1990, and destabilized and brought down the democratically elected governments of Guatemala, Chile, Greece, and Haiti – all acts entirely outside the parameters of international law.

It has given and still gives total support to the Turkish government's campaign of genocide against the Kurdish people. It describes the Kurdish resistance forces in Turkey as 'terrorists' whereas it referred to its own vicious Contra force in Nicaragua as 'freedom fighters'. Its 'covert' action against Nicaragua was declared by the International Court of Justice in The Hague to be in clear breach of International Law.

Over the last five years the UN has passed five resolutions with overwhelming majorities demanding that the US stop its embargo on Cuba. The US has ignored all of them. All UN resolutions criticizing Israel have been ignored, not only by Israel but also by the US, which turns a blind eye to Israel's nuclear capability and shrugs off Israel's oppression of the Palestinian people.

The US possesses of course quite a handy nuclear capability itself. I would say it outstrips Saddam's ability to kill 'every man, woman and child on earth' by quite a few miles. If that wasn't enough, it also has substantial chemical arsenals and has recently rejected two UN inspectors, one Cuban and one Iranian. It also reserves the right to deny access to certain 'national security' zones. They are closed to inspection as 'inspection may pose a threat to the national security interests of the US'.

Isn't Saddam Hussein saying something like that?

George Kennan, head of the US State Department, setting out the ground rules for US foreign policy in a 'top secret' internal document in 1948, said: 'We will have to dispense with all sentimentality and day-dreaming and our attention will have to be concentrated everywhere on our immediate national objectives. We should cease to talk about vague and unreal objectives such as human rights, the raising of living

[237]

standards and democratization. The day is not far off when we are going to have to deal in straight power concepts. The less we are hampered by idealistic slogans the better.' Kennan was an unusual man. He told the truth.

I'm sure you would agree that historical perspective is of the first importance and that a proper detachment is a crucial obligation which devolves upon leaders of men.

Anyway, this is your ally, with whom you are locked in a moral embrace.

Oh, by the way, meant to mention, forgot to tell you, we were all chuffed to our bollocks when Labour won the election.

Acknowledgements

PROSE

'A Note on Shakespeare' (1950), copyright © 1998 by Harold Pinter. On *The Birthday Party* I (30 March 1958) first published *Kenyon Review*, Vol. III, No. 3 Summer 1981, copyright © 1981 by Neabar Investments Ltd. Martin Esslin's 'Note' first published *Kenyon Review*, Vol. III, No. 3 Summer 1981, copyright © 1981 by Martin Esslin. On *The Birthday Party* II (October 1958), *The Play's the Thing*, copyright © 1958 by Neabar Investments Ltd. 'Writing for the Theatre' (speech made by Harold Pinter at the National Student Drama Festival in Bristol, 1962) first published by Methuen & Co in *Harold Pinter Plays One*, 1962, copyright © 1962, 1964 by Neabar Investments Ltd. 'Mac' (1966) first published by Emanuel Wax for Pendragon Press 1968, copyright © 1968 by Neabar Investments Ltd. 'Hutton and the Past' (1969) first published as 'Memories of Cricket' in the *Daily Telegraph Magazine*, 16 May 1969, copyright © 1969 by Neabar Investments Ltd. 'On Being Awarded the 1970 German Shakespeare Prize' (1970) first published by Methuen & Co. in *Harold Pinter Plays Three*, 1970, copyright © 1970 by Neabar Investments Ltd. 'Arthur Wellard' (1981) first published in *Summer Days*, edited by Michael Meyer, Methuen London, 1981, copyright © 1981 by Neabar Investments Ltd. 'Jimmy' first published by Pendragon Press, 1984, copyright © 1984 by Harold Pinter. 'Beckett' first published in *Beckett at Sixty* by Calder and Boyars, 1967, copyright © 1967 by Harold Pinter. 'Samuel Beckett', a televised tribute to Samuel Beckett, BBC2, 1990, copyright © 1998 by Harold Pinter. 'Speech of thanks for the David Cohen British Literature Prize for 1995' privately printed by Faber and Faber, 1995, copyright © 1995 by Harold Pinter. 'On the screenplay of *A la recherche du temps perdu*' first published in *The Proust Screenplay* in 1978 by Eyre Methuen in association with Chatto and Windus, copyright © 1978 by Neabar Investments Ltd. 'Harold Pinter and Michael Billington in conversation at the National Film Theatre' (26 October 1996), copyright © 1998 by Harold Pinter and Michael Billington. 'Writing, Politics and *Ashes to Ashes*', interview with Harold Pinter by Mireia Aragay and Ramon Simó, Universitat de Barcelona, Departement de Filologia Anglesa i Alemanya (Barcelona, 6 December 1996), copyright © 1998 by Harold Pinter and Mireia Aragay.

PROSE FICTION

'Kullus' (1949) previously published in *Poems*, Enitharmon Press, 1968, copyright © 1968 by Neabar Investments Ltd. 'Latest Reports from the

Stock Exchange' (1953) first published in the *Sunday Times*, 2 February 1997, copyright © 1997 by Harold Pinter. 'The Black and White' (1954–55) first published in *Transatlantic Review*, Summer 1966, copyright © 1966 by Neabar Investments Ltd. 'The Examination' (1955) first published in *Encounter* in 1960 and subsequently in *The Collection and The Lover*, Methuen & Co., 1963, copyright © 1963 by Neabar Investments Ltd. 'Tea Party' (1963) first published in *Playboy*, January 1965, copyright © 1965 by Neabar Investments Ltd. 'The Coast' (1975) first published in *Transatlantic Review*, May 1976, copyright © 1976 by Neabar Investments Ltd. 'Problem' (1976) first published in *Transatlantic Review*, June 1977, copyright © 1977 by Neabar Investments Ltd. 'Lola' (1977) first published in *The New Review*, Vol. 3 No. 36, copyright © 1977 by Neabar Investments Ltd. 'Short Story' (1995) first published in *London Magazine*, October/November 1995, Vol. 35 Nos. 7 & 8, copyright © 1995 by Harold Pinter. 'Girls' (1995) first published in the *Sunday Times* and *Granta*, 1995, copyright © 1995 by Harold Pinter.

POETRY

'School Life' (1948) copyright © 1998 by Neabar Investments Ltd. 'At the Palace of the Emperor at Dawn' (1949), 'Once, in a Ventriloquist Evening' (1949), 'Others of You' (1951), 'Episode' (1951) and 'The Irish Shape' (1951) first published in *Ten Early Poems* by Greville Press Pamphlets, copyright © 1992 by Neabar Investments Ltd. 'New Year in the Midlands' (1950), 'The Midget' (1950), 'Christmas' (1950), 'Chandeliers and Shadows' (1950), 'Hampstead Heath' (1951), 'I Shall Tear Off my Terrible Cap' (1951), 'A Glass at Midnight' (1951), 'Book of Mirrors' (1951), 'The Islands of Aran Seen from the Moher Cliffs' (1951), 'Jig' (1952), 'The Anaesthetist's Pin' (1952), 'You in the Night' (*c.* 1952), 'The Second Visit' (*c.* 1952), 'A Walk by Waiting' (1953), 'Poem' (1953), 'The Task' (1954), 'The Error of Alarm' (1956), 'Daylight' (1956), 'Afternoon' (1957), 'A View of the Party' (1958), 'The Table' (1963), 'Poem' (1964) and 'All of That' (1970) first published in *Poems*, Enitharmon Press, 1968, copyright © 1968 by Neabar Investments Ltd. 'The Drama in April' (1952), 'Camera Snaps' (1952) and 'Poem' (1971) first published in *Poems*, Enitharmon Press, 1972 (second edition), copyright © 1972 by Neabar Investments Ltd. 'Later' (1974) first published in *The New Review*, Vol. 2 No. 23, copyright © 1976 by Neabar Investments Ltd. 'Poem' (1974) first published in *Aquarius* No. 7, copyright © 1974 by Neabar Investments Ltd. 'I Know the Place' (1975) and 'Paris' (1975) first published in *Bananas*, No. 9 Winter 1977, copyright © 1977 by Neabar Investments Ltd. 'The Doing So' (1977) and 'Message' (1977) first published in *The New Review*, Vol. 4 No. 39, copyright © 1977 by Neabar Investments Ltd. 'Denmark Hill' (1977) first published in *Collected Poems and Prose*, Faber and Faber, 1991, copyright © 1991 by Neabar Investments

Ltd. 'Joseph Brearley 1909–1977 (Teacher of English)' (1977) and 'Poem' (1986) first published in *Soho Square II*, Bloomsbury, 1989, copyright © 1977 by Neabar Investments Ltd. 'The Ventriloquists' (1981) first published in *London Magazine*, April/May 1982, copyright © 1982 by Neabar Investments Ltd. 'Poem' (1981) first published in the *Times Literary Supplement*, 15 May 1981, copyright © 1981 by Neabar Investments Ltd. 'Ghost' (1983) first published in the *Times Literary Supplement*, 4 November 1983, copyright © 1983 by Neabar Investments Ltd. 'Before They Fall' (1983) first published in the *Observer*, 22 January 1984, copyright © 1984 by Neabar Investments Ltd. 'It Is Here' (1990) first published in the *Times Literary Supplement*, 2 February 1990, copyright © 1990 by Neabar Investments Ltd. 'American Football' first published in the *Socialist*, 15–28 January 1992, copyright © 1992 by Neabar Investments Ltd. 'God' first published in the *Guardian*, 24 December 1994, copyright © 1994 by Neabar Investments Ltd. 'Poem' first published in the *Guardian*, 17 January 1995, copyright © 1995 by Neabar Investments Ltd. 'Cricket at Night' first published in the *Guardian*, 3 June 1995, copyright © 1995 by Neabar Investments Ltd. 'The Other Guy' first published in the *Guardian*, 15 July 1995, copyright © 1995 by Neabar Investments Ltd. 'Order' first published in the *Guardian*, 12 September 1996, copyright © 1996 by Neabar Investments Ltd. 'The Old Days' first published in the *Observer*, 29 September 1996, copyright © 1996 by Neabar Investments Ltd. 'Death (Births and Deaths Registration Act 1953)' first published in the *Times Literary Supplement*, 10 October 1997, copyright © 1997 by Neabar Investments Ltd. 'Requiem for 1945' first published in the *Sunday Times*, 30 May 1999, copyright © 1999 by Neabar Investments Ltd.

POLITICS

'The US Elephant Must Be Stopped' first published in the *Guardian*, 5 December 1987, copyright © 1987 by Harold Pinter. 'Eroding the Language of Freedom' first published in *Sanity*, March 1989, copyright © 1989 by Harold Pinter. 'Oh, Superman' from *Opinion*, shown on Channel 4, 31 May 1990, copyright © 1998 by Harold Pinter. 'Blowing up the Media' first published in *Index on Censorship*, 5 May 1992, copyright © 1992 by Harold Pinter. 'The US and El Salvador' first published in the *Observer*, 28 March 1993, copyright © 1993 by Harold Pinter. 'Pinter: Too Rude for Convicts' first published in the *Guardian*, 9 June 1995, copyright © 1995 Alan Travis, *Guardian*. 'Caribbean Cold War' first published in *Red Pepper*, May 1996, copyright © 1996 by Harold Pinter. Quotations from *Silent Revolution* reproduced from *The Silent Revolution: The Rise of Market Economics in Latin America* by permission of Cassell, Wellington House, 125 Strand, London WC2R OBB. '*Mountain Language* in Haringey' first published in the *Guardian*, 21 June 1996, by Duncan Campbell, copyright ©